# Young Warriors

# Young Warriors:
# Youth Politics, Identity and
# Violence in South Africa

Monique Marks

WITWATERSRAND UNIVERSITY PRESS

Witwatersrand University Press
1 Jan Smuts Avenue
2000 Johannesburg
South Africa

First published 2001


ISBN 1-86814-370-8

Cover artwork: Paul Weinberg / South Photographs
Typeset by: Brigitte Plisnier, B-Complex
Printed and bound by: NBD, Drukkery Street, Goodwood, Cape Town


Distributed in North America by:

Transaction Publishers,
Rutgers University,
35 Berrue Circle,
Piscataway, NJ 08854 USA

Tel: (732)445-2280
Fax: (732)445-3138
for orders (US only):
toll free 888-999-6778

# Table of contents

# Dedication

This book is dedicated to Vuyani Mabaxa who was murdered in October 1991. Vuyani was a key youth activist in Diepkloof through the '80s and early '90s and, in many ways, was responsible for making this research a reality. He not only helped me gain access to the research setting, he also became a friend who gained my trust and deepest respect. Vuyani's life and death provided an inspiration for completing this book.

# Acknowledgements

I would like to express my deepest gratitude to the youth of Diepkloof whom this book is about. They willingly bestowed their trust, friendship and encouragement without which this book would never have been written. There are two people from Diepkloof that I would particularly like to mention. First, my greatest thanks go to Musa Manganyi for his assistance throughout the time I spent in Diepkloof, for engaging openly with me about my research findings, for reading an early draft of the manuscript and contributing his own ideas, clarifications, and points of contention. Second, Makgane Thabojane (who contributed the foreword to this book) was really my first point of contact in Diepkloof. After initially 'checking me out', he became a key reference person and helped me to understand the dynamics of Diepkloof and youth politics in general. Makgane gave me the jostle I needed when I was hesitant about publishing the manuscript as a book.

There are also two people in the Sociology Department at the University of Natal that I would like to mention. First, Belinda Bozzoli (who initially supervised this work) provided constant encouragement, intellectual guidance, and a genuine interest in the youth who contributed to this book. In particular, Belinda was a great source of strength to me when I heard that Vuyani had been killed. Second, I would like to thank Jon Hyslop for always encouraging me in my work, both when I was based at the University of the Witwatersrand and later when I moved to the University of Natal. I can honestly say that without Jon's scholarly and personal generosity, I may not have had the fortitude to complete this book.

Above all, I would like to thank Muff Andersson for taking on the daunting task of editing this book. Muff went far beyond the role of editor in working on the manuscript. She provided an early vision of what the book could look like and, in the later stages, helped in the design and layout of the book. Muff constantly amazed me with her diverse skills and energy.

Finally, I would like to thank Hyreath Anderson and Wits University Press for believing that this book has value as a worthwhile publication.

*Monique Marks*

# Foreword

The involvement of youth in politics in Diepkloof began with a concern about how our parents were being exploited in terms of rent. In 1980, during an assembly at Bopa Senatla High School in Diepkloof, a certain Mokgomotsi Mogodire took over the reins. He disconnected the telephone and addressed 500 of us regarding the high rentals. We immediately agreed action was required. We marched to other high schools and converged at the local municipal offices, which were effectively stopped from operating. When I excitedly reported the incident to my parents that night, they pointed out that they paid the rent, not me. This only motivated me to continue our struggle.

When Mokgomotsi recruited me into the Congress of South African Students a while later, I immediately agreed based on the experiences of that day at Bopa Senatla. Our preoccupation at the time was to build an organisation, to ensure that a solid base was established, to sustain the organisation and to protect leadership. A dynamic and coherent student movement was established, nationally and in Soweto. Diepkloof was a part of the whole. We achieved a presence in all high schools in Soweto and a leadership core emerged. In 1984 we were detained, 14 days before our end-of-year matric exams, and were held for four months. Once this happened, a new layer of leadership had to be developed in Diepkloof and  the 1985 Detachment was formed.

The strategy of the detachment was straightforward: organise people around issues that directly affect them; build sufficient layers of leadership to ensure continuity; and take over the governance of our schools. At the school level, this translated into the need to form strong SRCs and PTSAs which gave us the ability to direct and control school periods and times and, more important, a schooling system that was responsive to the needs of students.

At the community level, the strategy translated into effective consumer, rent and bus boycotts. To achieve this meant forging alliances with the women's movements. A strong and committed group of activists came to the fore, some of whom are mentioned in this book. These activists included many powerful women – Ma Moloise, Thandi Mazibuko, Margaret Stoffel, Norah Sono, Nhlanhla Motlhanke, Ohara and Mpule come immediately to mind – and members of the teaching fraternity led by the principals Bravo Maseki, Mguni and Manota. The civic movement at the centre of mobilisation and struggle in Diepkloof, along with Isaac Mogase and resources from Nthato Motlana, were critical in the role they played in mobilising the elderly as part of this movement. Lastly, the small businesses, which included tavern owners, made their limited resources available to our noble cause. We never stopped to think about what they did and to thank them. The youth in Diepkloof were faced with many obstacles, but these obstacles only made our movement stronger. Aside from the police and the army, the problem of gangsterism plagued us from the mid '80s. When confronted with gangsterism in the form of Kabasa in 1985 and 1986, Jackrollers in 1988 and 1989, and Kabasa again in 1989, we were more than determined, ready and organised to take them head on and win. Despite police taking the side of the gangsters, the reality that 6 300 students of Diepkloof were mobilised and the street committees intact, meant that the township was liberated from such elements.

Linked to this campaign was a focus on agents of the state machinery in the form of police and their families, councillors and informers. I remember the students once indicating during a mass meeting that Musa (one of the detachment's leaders) was also the son of a policeman (who was based in Giyane in the Northern Province). We undertook to ensure that his father never visited the family, that all contact with him be terminated immediately, that he be informed never to send any money to the family – which undertaking was accepted and has prevailed up to this day. Remember, too, that Azapo leader Muntu Myeza resided in Diepkloof. So did Dan Khabedi, an Azapo activist. In all these struggles, a conscious effort was made to recruit and organise a black consciousness movement although black consciousness was an ideology that never took root in Diepkloof.

When Vuyani Mabaxa (a central character in this book and one of Diepkloof's heroes) came to our detachment and talked about this white woman, Monique, who wanted to be part of our processes, our first concern was about security. 'Are you sure she hasn't been deployed by the security forces?' we asked him. He had done some basic checks and indicated that she was okay. But we decided to continue doing checks. If we were having a meeting, we would plan to meet at Point A, then move to Point B, then to Point C. We were happy as long as she arrived at Point A, not at Point C, as only the leadership core knew Point C.

Our second concern was that the information Monique was gathering should not be exposed – some was highly classified. Eventually we decided that anyone could infiltrate our detachment and get the same information and, as such, the same security consciousness prevailed. We agreed to accept her. Besides, Vuyani was highly regarded in our detachment.

Once we had spoken to Monique, we were relatively comfortable. She was a comrade herself and we were happy with her struggle credentials. We were very clear about the need to record the history of our struggle and our wish to contribute to that process. However, we didn't have the time, skills, capacity or resources to do such work on a continuous basis, and knew there were gaps in our history. Some MK comrades from Diepkloof made a big contribution to our struggle. I was personally responsible, among others, for building up early student and youth structures. We knew the difficulty of trying to understand what happened before our time and of the history that was being lost – future generations were being robbed of valuable lessons.

We made sure Vuyani was the link person throughout the project. He was Monique's mentor, and judged what she could be exposed to. We gave him carte blanche, and he literally exposed her to everything.

Although this book is not about Vuyani, he worked very closely with Monique and was something of a symbol for us so I want to write more words about him. Vuyani was part of our leadership core. He had survived many periods of detention. We placed him at the strategic level of being a continuous leader. Detention usually helped the state to build up some sort of dossier on an individual. It provided the means for the state to 'understand' the activist. They hadn't been able to do that with Vuyani. I'm sure he intimidated them. He was tall, with a good bearing – he had a heroic stature – and he was physically strong. As a person, he was dynamic and intelligent, but also humble, able to understand and to contextualise.

He didn't come from a particularly political family. His parents were both ordinary members of Nehawu – a trade union affiliate in the public sector. But Vuyani was one of those all-rounders, involved in every aspect of struggle from his teens until the day he died in his mid-twenties at the hands of the security forces. Shortly after the banning of Cosas, he became a full-time activist and, after one of his periods in detention, an organiser at Nehawu. He didn't have a personal life. He was committed to the core. Vuyani was a political fanatic. He lived politics Monday to Monday. He didn't have time for social events – he was too serious.

Vuyani knew the dangers of being politically active and some say he predicted that he would be killed. Three weeks before he died, another comrade – his friend Papo Manyakalle – was killed, found in the outside toilet of a friend's home with a fatal head wound and a 9 mm pistol at his side. Vuyani and all of us disputed the suicide theory. After that, Vuyani started to get nervous, more scared than normal and not himself. He had written the poem 'Just in case I die', and I think he must have had a vision of his own death or seen it as inevitable. But it was because of these extraordinary qualities that Vuyani displayed – his dedication and commitment – that he became a symbol to us. A number of people had been assassinated, through gangsterism, police action, and in detention. We decided to build a memorial figure for all of those fallen comrades, using Vuyani's image. This figure still stands in one of Diepkloof's open fields.

As usual, after anything significant that happened, the detachment analysed and assessed and restrategised. Vuyani's death was a turning point for us. Even the underground structures felt it was time to come out in open defiance. At the funeral, a message was read in the service explaining that Vuyani was second in command of armed activities in Diepkloof, and it was the duty of his unit to avenge him. The state was trying to create the perception that it had killed our commander. The message declared, 'You've got our second in command', and the battle was to be accelerated. That was a breakthrough.

At the funeral, security was very tight. An AK47 and Scorpion were used to salute Vuyani in open public and, despite the police searching all people individually, they could not capture those arms. It was like watching a movie as an ambulance was used to hide the arms for safety, as if carrying a pregnant woman from the graveyard to hospital. The police were shocked by the sophistication displayed and by the masses of our people who celebrated the public presence of the people's army.

Did we allow ourselves to feel grief? Yes and no. Death was part of our lives. We had a sense of ourselves as being continuous. We believed that whenever someone fell, there must be others standing. We were preoccupied with not losing too many, and also with not allowing statistics to weigh against us only but also against the state.

Were we normal youth? I don't think so. We were forced to mature and be responsible long before our time. The detachment, for example, despite being made up of very young people, gave leadership around all issues affecting the community – even marital and family disputes were brought to our attention for amicable resolution. Possibly you could say we jumped our life as youths. When I stepped down as general secretary of Nehawu in 1988, I said two things: 'First, there's a need for a different rhythm in leadership after sufficient policy development into the stage of implementation. Second, I have clearly missed the period of my youth. I need to catch up, to regain my own life, both personally and politically.'

I still interact with some of the student and youth organisations, and obviously with trade union organisations too. But the challenges to youth are different now. A direct comparison between then and now would be misleading. In those days, just being a shop steward was a sign of commitment and accepting a leadership position in the youth movement took additional commitment and sacrifice. Recently, however, we've seen in the trade union movement that some see being a shop steward as a career opportunity. The same happens in the student and youth movements. Back then, we had democratic centralism and collective leadership. We had to work hard to produce true leadership, and even more important, to have layers of alternative leadership to replace in the case of death or detention. Out of pure necessity, the leadership plan was paramount. The context has changed now and one finds there is often this link to careerism and individual fame.

In those days there was a connection between the graduation from high-school leader to youth leader and/or to tertiary leader. There was an interconnectedness between the organisations, an inter-dependence. Today that's not there. The organisations are poles apart. Our organisations found common cause in our strategies and tactics. Today that doesn't exist. The organisations are not as coherent and cohesive. Today, too, I have noticed this preoccupation with resources: 'We can't do this because we don't have the resources'. For us, resources were never a problem – although we didn't have a thing. Somehow we managed to bring out T-shirts and pamphlets, and to organise defence in a very sophisticated way. The community would always participate and so too did a network of resource organisations, NGOs and international support – which it must be said do not exist today. We never discussed whether we would survive, that crime was a problem, but made it our duty to eradicate such evils.

In the different context of today, we see that careerism and blind allegiance to the youth movement is killing its dynamism and ability to think independently. A key lesson that was relevant both then and now is this: *if you are building a popular movement, it has to be mass-rooted and programme-led.*

This book explains just how we, in Diepkloof, succeeded in doing that.

**Makgane Thobejane**
**Labour Relations Specialist: City of Johannesburg**
**Formerly Nehawu General Secretary**
**Formerly 1985 Detachment, Diepkloof**

**August 2000**

# List of abbreviations

| | |
|---|---|
| ANC | African National Congress |
| ANCYL | African National Congress Youth League |
| Ayco | Alexandra Youth Congress |
| Azapo | Azanian People's Organisation |
| Azasm | Azanian Students' Movement |
| Case | Community Agency for Social Enquiry |
| Codesa | Congress for a Democratic South Africa |
| Cosas | Congress of South African Students |
| Cosatu | Congress of South African Trade Unions |
| CPSA | Communist Party of South Africa |
| Cosaw | Congress of South African Writers |
| DET | Department of Education and Training |
| HRC | Human Rights Commission |
| MDM | Mass Democratic Movement |
| MK | Umkhonto we Sizwe |
| Nehawu | National Education, Health and Allied Workers' Union |
| Nicro | National Institute for Crime Prevention and Rehabilitation of Offenders |
| NP | National Party |
| Nusas | National Union of South African Students |
| NYC | National Youth Commission |
| PWV | Pretoria-Witwatersrand-Vereeniging |
| Sabswa | South African Black Social Workers' Association |
| SACP | South African Communist Party |
| SADF | South African Defence Force |
| Sadtu | South African Democratic Teachers' Union |
| Sansco | South African National Students' Congress |
| SAP | South African Police |
| Sasco | South African Students' Congress |
| Sayco | South African Youth Congress |
| SDU | Self-defence Unit |
| Sosco | Soweto Students' Congress |
| Soyco | Soweto Youth Congress |
| SRC | Students' Representative Council |
| TRC | Truth and Reconciliation Commission |
| UDF | United Democratic Front |

# Dramatis personae

**BHEKI:** Born 1960, Diepkloof. His violent and abusive father abandoned the family when Bheki was young. Bheki never went to school because his family was too poor to send him. When he was 12, he was accused of killing a policeman. (He denies this.) He left South Africa for Zambia where he joined Umkhonto we Sizwe (MK). In 1993, Bheki was 'very ashamed' of being unable to read or write. He lived in a shack with his brother in Mandela Village. He appeared to be supporting his mother, brother and sister from the sale of bread, milk and sweets. They lived in extreme poverty. 'Sometimes we go for two weeks eating a porridge with a tea, or with water,' he told me. Bheki's claim of being an activist was disputed by other activists who said he never attended meetings. Some residents thought he was involved with a gang, possibly linked to Inkatha. Bheki also claimed to be a regular churchgoer. His hopes were to attend school eventually and to get a 'proper job'.

**CHRIS:** Born 1971, Hammanskraal (Northern Transvaal). In 1988, his family moved to Diepkloof where they bought a house. His mother was a domestic worker; his father was unemployed when he died in the early '90s. Chris lived with his mother and younger brother. He didn't get involved politically until he completed his matric in 1991. Despite his inexperience with politics, he was elected publicity officer for the African National Congress Youth League (ANCYL) branch in 1992. His mother was unhappy about this, thinking the comrades 'maybe do like hijacking and all that and [Chris] ends up in jail'. At the time I interviewed him, he was doing a post-matric course at an adult education centre. He wanted to enter a technical college at some point, but was 'worried about the problem of money'.

**JABU:** Born 1976, Diepkloof. His parents had owned a house in Sophiatown. In Diepkloof, they were forced to rent one. Both were unemployed (although his mother had previously been a domestic worker and his father a bus driver, before being seriously injured in an accident). Jabu lived with his parents and four younger siblings. They were supported by other relatives. Jabu formally joined the Congress of South African Students (Cosas) in 1990. He was a serious and active member.

**LILLIAN:** Born 1974, Diepkloof. Her parents had moved from Sophiatown to Kliptown to Diepkloof in the early '70s. When she was in junior school, she lived with her grandmother in Dobsonville. At the time of interviewing, she was doing matric at a 'fly-by-night' college in town. She never got her results. After her father's death, Lillian lived in a rented house with her mother, brother, sister and sister's child. Her mother was a pensioner and her sister, who worked as a shopfitter, supported the family. Lillian got involved after the unbannings in February 1990 when she was elected African National Congress (ANC) branch treasurer. Her sudden withdrawal from youth activism a few years later resulted, I suspect, from her pregnancy.

**LINDI:** Born 1975, Diepkloof. Lindi had spent four years of her life with her grandmother in Balfour near Durban. When I met her she lived with thirteen family members. Her parents were unemployed. Her sister, who worked at Baragwanath, appeared to be supporting the family. Lindi and her friend Thandi joined the ANCYL in 1991 – in response to the murder of Vuyani Mabaxa. Her parents were supportive because they thought 'the comrades are fighting for freedom'. When asked what apartheid meant to her, Lindi said she did not know because she had not been in the organisation for a long time. Despite the fact that she had failed two years at school, she hoped to become a doctor.

**LUMKILE:** Born 1967, Diepkloof. His parents were originally from Alexandra. His father died in a car accident when Lumkile was very young. When I interviewed him, he lived with his mother – a cashier – and elder brother in a house belonging to his mother. In 1991, his mother joined the ANC Women's League. Lumkile joined Cosas in 1985. He was a respected local youth leader at the time. He wrote matric in detention in 1988. He never got his results. Disillusioned and fearing police harassment, he never went back to school. Central in the 'war' with the gangs, Lumkile was shot in 1990 by a member of the Jackrollers. His injuries meant he could not do heavy manual work so he had to get part-time jobs and was often unemployed. He admitted to owning a firearm but said he used it in a 'disciplined manner' for political gain only. Community members accused him of rape, murder and theft. He was killed in one of the gang wars in the township in late 1993.

**LUMKO:** Born 1977, Diepkloof. His parents came from Alexandra. They separated in 1979. When I met him, Lumko was in Standard 6. He had been an active member of Cosas since the late '80s but was not in any leadership position. He lived in a rented house with his mother, grandmother and four siblings. His mother worked as a cleaner at the local municipality, his sister as a cashier at a supermarket. He had failed three years of primary school, but hoped to become a lawyer one day.

**MUSI:** Born 1975, Diepkloof. His parents had also come from Alexandra. In Diepkloof, they lived in a rented house with their five children. Musi's father worked for the Putco bus company as a clerk, his mother was a nurse. They did not support their son's activism. Musi got very involved in youth politics in the '80s. He was an executive member of the local Cosas branch. Politically astute and articulate, Musi had never failed a year of school. He was writing matric and planned to study at university. Of all the youth I interviewed, Musi struck me as the only one with a likely chance of getting tertiary education.

**NAMEDI:** Born 1971, Diepkloof. His mother, separated from his father (a policeman), was from Swaziland. She worked as a part-time domestic worker and lived with Namedi, his brother, three sisters and their three children in a rented house. Namedi was attending a technical college in Zola, a part of Soweto. He hoped to become a mechanic. Probably due to his activism, he failed his final exams at the end of 1991 and then again at the end of 1992. He joined Cosas in 1985, became a respected youth leader and was elected as the ANCYL Diepkloof branch's first chair in 1991. The following year, he was elected on to the Soweto sub-regional ANCYL executive. Because of his exceptional political insight and extensive experience, he became one of my 'key informants'.

**NIKA:** Born 1970, Diepkloof. He lived with his father's sister in Witbank until 1987. He completed Standard 9, but left Witbank after being shot by police 'for being involved in politics'. When I met him, he lived with his mother (originally from Sophiatown) and stepfather. He disliked his stepfather who frequently beat his wife and stepchildren. In Diepkloof, Nika enrolled at a secretarial college but had to pull out 'because of lack of funds'. He was fired from part-time work at the Market Theatre after 'a racial confrontation with a white customer'. Although he presented himself as politically astute and was a regular at ANCYL meetings, he was later accused of being a spy. Some activists believed he was informing the police about Vuyani Mabaxa's activities. He had been seen at the house of a policeman the night before Vuyani's death. Namedi established that Nika had been forced to leave Witbank by activists there as he was suspected of being a state agent. Nika left Diepkloof shortly after Vuyani's assassination.

**SELLO:** Born 1973, Diepkloof. His parents were from Sophiatown. Sello lived in a shack in People's Village by choice – he didn't get on with his father. He attended a local high school but dropped out after Standard 7. This was largely because he had spent much of his life in the mid- and late '80s in hiding and a spell in detention. When I met him he was working from his shack as a hairdresser. In the early '90s, he was a member of the ANCYL but not a leader. In late 1992, his girlfriend had a baby. After this, he began the business of seeking formal employment to maintain his child.

**SENATSO:** Born 1966, Diepkloof. In 1972 his mother was a domestic worker in Booysens and Senatso lived with her in the 'servants'' quarters. In 1977 she got another job in Mondeor. Senatso was sent to live in Kliptown with friends of his father. He then moved back to Diepkloof where he lived with his grandmother and started primary school. His grandmother, a pensioner, could not afford the fees. By the time Senatso was 21, he had not completed Standard 5. Because of his age, he was not allowed to continue his schooling. In the interim, his father deserted the family. His mother be-came an alcoholic and was unable to care for her children in any way. In 1986, Senatso was detained for 11 months. When he was released, he found a job as a carpenter and earned R10 a week – which was less than he paid for transport. He was forced to leave the job and his grandmother asked him to leave her home. When I met him, he was living in the homes of various friends but had no real 'base'. He joined Cosas in 1985 and was still an active member of the ANCYL in the early '90s. He hoped to go back to school and to train as a mechanic.

**SIPHO:** Born 1963, Thabagona (Northern Transvaal). He moved to Diepkloof in 1988 to stay with his grandmother after being harassed as an activist in the Northern Transvaal, and was eventually detained from 1986 to 1988. When I met him, he was staying in a shack at the back of his cousin's house because his grandmother had died. He had completed his matric at a private school, sponsored by an older brother. Actively involved in youth poli-tics, he was elected chairperson of the Diepkloof ANCYL branch in 1992. He worked for six months selling books for Phambile Books in Johannesburg but was retrenched and was unable, afterwards, to find work. He started to write poetry in detention and wanted to publish it through the Congress of South African Writers (Cosaw). However, he could not afford transport to meetings and workshops which were generally held in Johannesburg.

**THABO:** Born 1968, Alexandra. His family were forcibly removed and placed in Diepkloof. When I met him, Thabo lived with his mother – a do-mestic worker, two sisters, younger brother and his sisters' two children in a rented 'matchbox' house. His father worked as a shoe repairman until he died of a stroke in 1988. Thabo joined Cosas in 1985 and became a key youth leader. His parents did not support his political involvement. He believed this contributed to his father's stroke: 'He was an old man and he didn't know from day-to-day where I was sleeping, how I ate, and so on. So I felt very guilty when he died.' Thabo completed Standard 9 at a Diepkloof school. From 1985 onwards, he was detained for long periods of time on numerous occasions. On his release in 1988, he went back to school to complete his matric. He was unable to do so because of police harassment. He was unem-ployed at the time of interviewing. While he considered himself an activist, he seemed to have been involved in numerous criminal activities and was on trial for the murder of his sister's boyfriend.

**THAMI:** Born 1976, Diepkloof. His parents had moved there from Alexandra. He lived in a house with his parents and three other siblings. His father worked as a packer at Pick 'n Pay until he was retrenched in 1989. The family was supported by Thami's brother who had a job at Woolworths. His mother had never had a job. Thami said the only problem in his family was that his sisters 'drink a lot of liquor', which caused fights. When I met him, he was repeating Standard 9 and appeared to be disillusioned with the education system. He joined Cosas in the late '80s but was critical of some of the organisation's activities and the fact that some Cosas members had firearms. He did not regularly attend meetings of either Cosas or the ANCYL but participated in the collective action of youth organisations in Diepkloof, including acts of arson. He had never been arrested or detained, but spent a lot of time in hiding, particularly in the late '80s. He hoped to get his matric and eventually become a traffic officer.

**THANDEKA:** Born 1972, Orlando, Soweto. Her parents were originally from Pietersburg in the Northern Transvaal. Her father, of whose occupation Thandeka was unaware, died of an illness in 1988. Her mother made a living selling the insides of chickens in Dobsonville. Thandeka, her sister, and her sister's young child lived in People's Village. They moved to the squatter camp because they were both zoned (for some unknown reason) for a high school in Diepkloof and could not afford to commute daily from Dobsonville. There were days when Thandeka and her sister went without food. This made concentrating at school very difficult. When I met her, Thandeka was repeating Standard 7. After failing for the third time, she decided to leave school. She was unemployed and simply 'hung around' the squatter camp. She joined the Soweto Students' Congress (Sosco) in the late '80s and later the ANCYL. Thandeka was harassed by police on numerous occasions. While she was not a key youth activist in Diepkloof, she knew the township – particularly the squatter camps – very well. She became a 'reliable respondent' for me. Thandeka hoped at some stage to go back to school and eventually to become a nurse.

**THANDI:** Born 1976, Diepkloof. Her parents were from Ciskei. She lived with them, four siblings and an uncle in a rented 'matchbox' house. Her father worked as a butcher, her mother as a cleaner at Diepkloof prison. At the time of interviewing, Thandi was doing Standard 7. With Lindi, she joined Cosas in 1991 after Vuyani Mabaxa's murder. She was politically very naïve. She hoped to become a nurse after she left school.

**THEMBA:** Born 1975, Diepkloof. His mother was from Alexandra; he didn't know the origins of his father. His mother was a cleaner at the Department of Revenue, his father a factory worker at Chapelet Sweets. He lived with them in a house in Diepkloof. His parents had a stormy relationship. They often sent him off to stay with relatives in townships outside of Soweto. Themba attended school in Diepkloof and was doing Standard 7 when I met him. He was new to political activism, having joined Cosas in 1991, and seemed to have a poor understanding of South African politics and organisational functioning. He had 'many friends who come from jail because they stole a car and for housebreaking'. He was a regular church-goer and wanted to become a lawyer or a doctor.

**XOLILE:** Born 1965, Alexandra. In 1969, his family moved to Diepkloof. His parents and their five children lived in a rented house. His mother was a domestic worker and his father a repairman. Since both parents worked throughout his childhood, Xolile was mainly brought up by his grandmother. He left school in Standard 9 because 'as an activist I never had a good relationship with my teachers and principal'. He tried to complete his schooling at a private college in town but 'never succeeded in passing'. He had been looking for work since leaving school but was unemployed when I met him. He became involved in Cosas in 1986 and was a rank-and-file member well into the '90s.

**ZOLA:** Born 1973, Diepkloof. He lived in a rented house with his grandmother, two uncles and their wives. His mother lived in a shack in another zone of Diepkloof with her lover. His father had left his mother in 1979 and lived in a place called Sweetwater, some distance from Diepkloof. His father sold beer to make a living. The household was supported by one of the uncles. Zola's mother did not work since she was very ill and had a pacemaker. Zola was doing Standard 7. He had been active in Sosco since the mid-'80s and was an executive member of a sub-structure of the Diepkloof ANCYL. He spent most of the mid- to late '80s in hiding 'after the police came to look for him ... and hit [his] granny with a gun'. In mid-1992, Zola was being pursued by the police who believed he was in possession of weapons. This in fact was the case. In late 1992, he left South Africa and joined MK in one of the frontline states.

# When police shot dead this youth

# Soweto's schools exploded

**V**UYANI MABAXA bled to death on the edge of a rubbish-filled stream on Sunday, after a headlong dash from police. The police say he shot at them and they fired back. A dozen

# CHAPTER 1 — Why did Comrade Vuyani Mabaxa have to die?

## JUST IN CASE I DIE

Please forgive me
I must say these things:
Please forgive my enemies
Maybe their background is unfortunate,
I am a proud soldier of the movement.

I know I cannot survive forever
I know many of my fellow combatants will survive forever
Don't ask me why I know.

I know that freedom is around the corner.
I know that when freedom is around the corner
Many ununderstandable things happen.
Ask SWAPO and UNTAG
This is called transition (a very funny word né?).

I am very proud of the contribution I have made, though negligible
I have never been alone in this struggle.
I have never had any regrets.
I have found this struggle on
This struggle is on as I write this
And I will leave it on.
Oh no I will participate as an ancestor,
By the way I am an African.
I am not more African than others.

Our people have a communal background (History)
And I know a Communist future.
Pass my warm and childish greetings to the Young Lions.
And most of all to inkokheli zethu [our leaders]
Comrades N M R Mandela; O R Tambo; Joe Slovo; Harry Gwala
Peter Skosana and Jay Naidoo.

(Vuyani Mabaxa, 27 August 1991)

Less than two months after writing this poem, Vuyani Mabaxa was 'gunned down in cold blood during a headlong flight from police pursuers' (*The Weekly Mail,* 25 October 1991). Vuyani was killed on his way to a meeting on Sunday morning. It was 7.30 am on 13 October 1991. At the time of his death, the police claimed Vuyani was heavily armed and that they shot him in self-defence. However, eyewitnesses had a different story to tell. According to them:

> ... a powder-blue kombi had been waiting for him as he left his home. He tried to flee to the valley which separates Diepkloof's Zone 2 from Zone 6. Three policemen got out of the blue kombi and chased him on foot. The police were shooting at him as they ran. He was unarmed and when he reached the small stream running through the valley, he turned towards them and raised his hands to give himself up. The police responded with a hail of bullets which brought him down. As he lay there, a policeman fired at him at close range to try to finish him off. (*The Other Newsletter*, November 1991)

Just three weeks before, Papo Manyakale, Vuyani's close friend and comrade, died under peculiar circumstances. He was found dead in the outside toilet of his grandfather's home with a fatal bullet wound in his head. Both Papo and Vuyani had been key ANCYL leaders in Diepkloof, one of Soweto's many townships. As youth activists, both Vuyani and Papo had been known for their commitment to the liberation movement. They had a strong support base in the township.

Diepkloof erupted into a scene of violence and social disorder at the news of Vuyani's assassination. This was described by one of the press reports at the time:

> In Diepkloof, pupils at two local schools barricaded streets and set two cars and a lorry on fire after ransacking a house in the area. Pupils hijacked cars as they marched on the house of slain ANC Youth League leader Vuyani Mabaxa. They were protesting against his death. (*The Star*, 15 October 1991)

Vuyani's funeral brought together thousands of people from all over Soweto as well as many people (black and white) who were members of the democratic movement. T-shirts bearing Vuyani's face promised to 'take up the spear' and forward the struggle that Vuyani had 'left behind'.

# Who was Vuyani Mabaxa?

But who was Vuyani, and why did his death shatter an entire community? Vuyani had been a young community leader, a trade unionist, and was soon to be a young father. Since his school days he had devoted his life to struggling for democracy and for a better life for the people of his community. In the '80s, he was one of the young people in Diepkloof who had built up the youth movement associated with the United Democratic Front (UDF), the umbrella body constituting anti-apartheid organisations within South Africa that shared the vision of the banned African National Congress (ANC). After the ANC was unbanned in 1990, Vuyani played a key role in developing the ANC Youth League (ANCYL) branch in Diepkloof. He was also an active member of the South African Communist Party (SACP). He strongly believed in a future society where exploitation and oppression would cease to be a feature of the newly established democratic South Africa.

Vuyani was also a key activist in the local civic association formed in the mid-'80s. His formal working life was spent as a trade union organiser in the National Education, Health and Allied Workers' Union (Nehawu), currently one of the biggest Congress of South African Trade Unions' (Cosatu) affiliates in the public sector.

When I entered Diepkloof township as a researcher looking at the local youth resistance movement, Vuyani was the first person I was introduced to as a representative of this movement. He was a gate-keeper to this community, protecting its members from people like myself – 'outsiders' – who could potentially expose his fellow activists through malice or naïvety, and release information in an indiscriminate and insensitive manner. Vuyani quizzed me about my intentions and about my own commitment to the values and visions that his organisations represented. I was given the green light only when I shared my own commitment to the democratic movement, and explained my political involvement with organisations aligned to the same movement that shaped Vuyani's life and identity.

In the months to follow, I learned to understand Vuyani a little, and to respect him greatly. He not only assured my access to the two organisations that form the basis of this book – ANCYL and the Congress of South African Students (Cosas) – but also introduced his young fellow activists to the importance of research and sharing information. He did everything in his power to protect me as I entered and exited the township. He made me aware that as a white woman I could bring unwanted state attention both to myself and to the members of the organisations I was researching.

In the early '90s, it was unusual for white people to enter the township freely. Those who did were generally viewed as members of the security forces, or alternatively as part of the underground resistance movement. A week before his murder, Vuyani urged me to keep a low profile since he feared the police were suspicious that I was bringing arms into the township. For a long time after Vuyani was murdered, I lived with the guilt of believing that my presence in the township had brought unwarranted attention to him and that indirectly, therefore, I was responsible for his death. Vuyani's death devastated those who had known him, and inspired his friends and comrades to recommit themselves to the struggle for democracy to which he had devoted his life.

Why was Vuyani killed, and why did the youth of Diepkloof respond collectively with violence to his assassination? Vuyani spoke in his poem of the 'struggle' he 'found on' and 'left'. It was this very struggle, the fight for democracy and for equality, which threatened those who had a stake in the existing state structure. Vuyani's vision as a 'proud member of the movement' represented a hatred for a system that had given rise both to the structural and the direct violence experienced by the majority of the people of South Africa. Vuyani would not rest until this violence had been eradicated and a new system of governance instituted. It was this spirit of resistance that the state of the time tried to destroy by murdering Vuyani. The youth of Diepkloof refused to let this spirit of resistance die.

This book is concerned with understanding the emergence and subsequent career of a broad social movement – the Charterist youth movement – of which Vuyani and his 'young lions' were a part. The 'Charterist' social movement distinguished itself from other anti-apartheid or liberation movements in that its supporters and constituent organisations embraced the Freedom Charter,◊ a consultative document outlining the demands of South Africa's people for a democratic country. The Freedom Charter was adopted as the ANC's guiding document in 1955, and its vision was a democratic and non-racial South Africa. The Charterist social movement was by far the largest liberation movement within South Africa and was a major force for change in the '80s.

I argue that while the Charterist youth movement in Diepkloof was slow to develop, by the mid-'80s it was a strong social movement with a large social base, a coherent ideology, and well-planned campaigns and programmes of action. Paradoxically, perhaps, the high levels of state repression at the time served to strengthen this social movement and provided the impetus for a strong and committed leadership core. Like any social movement, however, there were problems that confronted the Charterist youth movement in Diepkloof. It was not always easy for youth leaders to control the mass social base, and sometimes there were discrepancies between the intentions and outcomes of collective action.

In the early '90s, these problems became more serious. In fact, the Charterist youth movement in Diepkloof (as elsewhere in the country) experienced a

---

◊ A copy of the Freedom Charter can be found in Appendix 2.

real decline. This coincided with the liberalisation of the political terrain as political organisations were unbanned in February 1990 and discussions for a negotiated settlement were set in motion. The social base of the movement altered as seasoned activists became disillusioned and new and less experienced youth moved into the organisations that constituted the social movement. Accompanying this changed social base and loss of proficient leaders was a less coherent ideology and a waning of well-organised campaigns and collective action. Collective violence, in particular, became more disordered and less judicious.

Through the voices of the young people who made up this social movement, the book will provide some insight as to how these youth organised themselves in a period of South African history when the consequence of being part of such organisations was literally life threatening. It examines the activities, ideologies and identities of activist youth in Diepkloof, and how these changed over time.

The book also hopes to provide insight into a major area of public concern: youth involvement in acts of collective violence. It asks a number of questions. How did the youth organise themselves to execute acts of violence? How did they justify these actions as participants in the liberation movement? Why did acts of collective violence become increasingly disorganised in the early '90s? In so doing, the book maintains that collective violence was an extension of other forms of more peaceful protest employed by these youth as participants in the liberation movement. While this violence was chaotic and poorly organised at times, it was always purposeful.

Finally, the book is concerned with understanding the identities that these youth created of themselves as 'soldiers' of peace and justice, and as 'comrades' in the struggle for national liberation.

This book is not about all youth in South Africa. It is the story of young men and women in one of Soweto's townships. And it is not about all youth in Diepkloof. Rather, it is only about those youth who identified themselves as part of a broader movement of people who aligned themselves with the Freedom Charter and the goals of the ANC.

While this book is about a particular group of youth, at a particular point in time, in just one of South Africa's many townships, it is a story of many others as well. It reflects the stories of thousands of men and women who are the products of the same organisations and struggles as the youth this book focuses on. It is also the story of many of South Africa's best-known leaders. It is the story of Paul Mashitile, currently Gauteng's MEC for Housing. It is the story of Cheryl Carolus, currently South Africa's ambassador to the UK. It is the story of Isaac Mogase, the first black mayor of Johannesburg. It is the story of Popo Molefe, currently the Premier of the North West. It is the story of Ignatius Jacobs, Gauteng's MEC for Education. It is indeed the story of many black South Africans who 'grew up' in the organisations of the ANC-led liberation movement.

This is not the only documentation of South African activist youth. Black youth resistance in South Africa has been a source of interest for many, particularly following the Soweto student uprisings in June 1976. After this incident, it became clear that the youth could not be ignored, but were a major force behind any change in South African society.

This book was conceived at a time when many in South Africa looked upon politicised youth as a menace, and began to speak about black youth in general as a 'lost generation', excluded from mainstream society, and with poor future prospects. Academics, journalists and even some political leaders who thought of black youth as a 'lost generation', fed into popular transitional anxieties. According to Seekings (1993), they painted a picture of black youth as 'posing a threat to "civilised" institutions and values'. The ability of South African society to incorporate 'the youth' into mainstream society was seen as a key test facing the project of democratisation in the early '90s.

But there were other concerns raised about black youth in the early '90s. They were labelled 'psychologically damaged', 'inherently violent' and 'anti-social' (Straker, 1992). As a result of this social exclusion, a general lack of opportunity, and a history of violent social engagement, they were believed to have a high propensity for involvement in violent crime (Mokwena, 1991; Leggett, 1999; Segal, Pelo & Rampa, 1999). It was assumed that youth engagement in violence and resistance was reactive and senseless, and that the same conditions gave rise simultaneously to both activism and criminality. Furthermore, it was believed that the boundary between political and criminal violence was extremely fluid, and that criminal gangs had become a 'family substitute' following the declining importance of political organisations.

This book has a completely different starting point. It pays special attention to the fact that the decline of political youth organisations in the early '90s was a contributing factor to the increase of criminal youth activity. It also reveals how the liberation movement's commitment to armed struggle and revolutionary violence was key to the spiralling culture of violence, and the unacceptably high levels of firearms in South African society. However, perhaps more importantly, it shows how young people in the liberation movement had highly conscious goals and motivations. They were not mindless menaces, but rather agents of change, symbols of a new future where future generations of black youth would experience political and social rights. Their collective activities, both violent and non-violent, cannot be seen as independent of the liberation social movement of which they were a key constituent, and which had clear objectives and related strategies. Of course this movement's activities had a number of unintended consequences, and they were not always well co-ordinated and organised. But their motivations were highly rational.

In exploring this, the book looks at how and why these youth joined political organisations. It examines how these organisations transformed from the '80s to the '90s as the politics of the day changed from liberation to negotiation, and how this in turn gave rise to new fears, hopes and frustrations for young activists, whose stories are told here. It concludes by exploring where black township youth find themselves today, what their new struggles are, and whether they have become (as some have proposed) today's criminals.

# CHAPTER 2

# White woman in 'Little Beirut'

When I decided to start this research, a number of people told me it was not a wise thing to do. They were worried that moving in and out of an African township, looking somewhat foreign, was extremely unsafe. Furthermore, this research was done during the transitional '90s when political violence had risen to an all-time high, characterised by massacres in the trains and informal settlements, drive-by shootings and random assassinations – particularly of ANC-aligned activists.

While the context of the townships during this period was an important consideration and did place some limits on the research, I was aware from the outset that a view from 'within' was essential. This was founded in a belief that collective action, collective violence and identities (the key concerns of this book) cannot be interpreted from structural contexts, nor from assumed psychological states of relative deprivation. As a result, this book is based on research from an 'insider' rather than an 'outsider' perspective.

## White – and a woman

How does one conduct research in areas plagued by intense political and criminal violence? Is it possible for a white person to do research effectively in black, particularly African, communities? Did the fact that I was white and a woman affect the research in any way? Readers are probably curious about these questions and I can only give my own subjective responses.

Diepkloof was renowned for its high levels of violence, both political and criminal. In Greater Soweto, Diepkloof was known as 'Little Beirut'. While the 'era of negotiations' brought with it a decline in the activities of the security forces, political violence took on a new and sinister face. Activists in the township continued to be 'eliminated'. There were constant threats of attack on the Diepkloof community from hostel-based Inkatha◊ supporters. Youth continued

---

◊ Inkatha has its roots as a Zulu cultural organisation in the early 1920s. It was constructed as a 'mass organisation' for Zulu people in the early 1970s. Inkatha was initially seen as falling within a similar political tradition to the ANC, although it was more rural and traditionally based. However, by the early '80s a serious tension emerged between Inkatha and ANC-aligned organisations over both strategy and ideology. By the mid-'80s, massive violent conflict, which some have called a civil war, erupted between the two movements in KwaZulu-Natal. In the early '90s, this violence spread to other places in the country such as Soweto and the East Rand. From the '80s, Inkatha also appeared to be increasingly aligning itself with the apartheid state.

to carry out acts of political violence in various forms. Diepkloof was also the turf of the Jackrollers, a notorious and extremely violent gang in Soweto.

Every time I entered the township, I felt an element of fear and apprehension. The threat of danger hindered the research in a real way. After a couple of months of moving in and out of the township at all hours, I had to stop attending evening meetings. Activists in Diepkloof could not assure my safety as I exited the township when it was dark, especially after Papo Mankyakale and Vuyani Mabaxa were murdered in late 1991. But I believed the research was important and ploughed on. People who live in the township make up a large proportion of the South African society and their day-to-day experiences of fear and anguish cannot be ignored. As researchers, we have to 'get our hands dirty'. We need to confront the realities of township life and place ourselves in the same precarious situations as the people about whom we write and theorise.

As a white person doing research in a black and highly politicised community, I met with mixed feelings about whether a white researcher can ever understand black research subjects adequately and whether it is possible to penetrate such communities. This is not something peculiar to the South African experience. A central concern among 'feminist' researchers, for example, is whether white women who call themselves feminist should do research on black women. Nkululeko, a black South African researcher, believed they should not. She says that 'knowledge cannot best be determined by alien researchers, who will always be laden with the trappings of their own history, values, culture and ideology, regardless of how progressive they may be' (1987: 89).

Edwards (1990), a white researcher who conducted and published interviews with Afro-Caribbean women in America, however, argues that while cross-racial research is difficult, it is not impossible. She believes that acknowledgement of her different structural position, and consequently her different assumptions about the world, facilitated her research project. At the root of these arguments lies the assumption that race in an almost unilinear way gives rise to a particular culture, meaning and values, and is consequently a primary category of identity.

My experience in Diepkloof contradicts these assumptions and has implications for white researchers in South Africa. The subjects of the research defined themselves primarily as 'comrades' and as 'youth', rather than as 'black'. My main point of entry into youth organisations was the fact that I was perceived as a 'comrade' (and, at 23, a 'youth') and therefore shared a common identity with the comrades in Diepkloof. The fact that I was white served more as a point of curiosity for the youth in Diepkloof than as a cause for alienation or suspicion.

On beginning my research, I met with two central youth figures in Diepkloof, Vuyani Mabaxa and Makgane Thobejane. Vuyani was an executive member of the ANCYL branch in Diepkloof and a central figure in youth politics in the area. Makgane was an executive member of the ANC branch and had been one of the founding members of youth organisations in Diepkloof. They both initially fired a number of questions at me. They were concerned that I would go into Diepkloof, take information, and make it public in any way I saw fit. This, they said, had been the case with many journalists. I had to explain that I was not a journalist, that I was interested in understanding the youth from their point of view, and that I had no intention of taking the booty and bolting. This seemed to put them more at ease, but they asked me about my political allegiances. I told them I was an ANC member, was on the executive of my local branch, and had been active in the South African Youth Congress (Sayco), an affiliate of the UDF, in the '80s. Both were greatly relieved to hear this. They said it 'made things different'. However, I still had to go through the organisational channels in Diepkloof and meet with the executives of Cosas and the ANCYL, and address their general membership, before I could begin my research. I gather a security check was also done on me by Vuyani and Makgane.

Engaging with social movements in the way that I did is somewhat controversial. Alain Touraine, a key social movement theorist, has suggested that researchers of social movements should be in solidarity with social movements, but should be independent of the organisations of struggle. In this case it became clear to me that to do the research I had to be part of the social movement concerned. The very fact that I could be identified as a 'comrade' and a 'youth' played a major role in assuring access to these organisations. My participatory role was essential in understanding the internal workings of these organisations and in developing trust and friendship among the activist youth in Diepkloof.

I came to believe that in order to do research on social movements in South Africa, particularly during highly politicised times, researchers have to take a clear stand on their ideological and political allegiances. An understanding of social movements from 'outside' will allow the researcher to answer certain questions about size, actions and 'organisational identity' (through the examination of pamphlets and documents), but does not adequately allow for studies that seek to deal with questions of individual subjectivity and identity. This 'allegiance' may raise questions around 'objectivity' and bias. These are real questions. But the benefits of being identified as an 'insider' (although I always remained an 'outsider' to the research setting, Diepkloof) far outweighed the costs.

There were both pros and cons to being a woman researcher. The main advantage, as was stated by a number of the youth I interviewed, was that they were less likely to assume I was a member of the police force. Both the young men and women in Diepkloof generally stereotyped women as being empathetic and nurturing. For this reason they conveyed very personal aspects of their experiences to me. Because I dressed fairly conservatively at times, councillors I interviewed assumed I could not be a member of any 'radical' organisation or the liberation movement.

There were disadvantages to being a woman as well. I was potentially an easy target for criminals in Diepkloof. Also, from time to time I felt sexually harassed by some of the male comrades. Once a young man followed me home and insisted I have sex with him. When I refused, he persisted and pestered me. Eventually I raised the problem with one of the ANCYL leaders, who then confronted him. The young man came to apologise and spoke to me about a number of personal problems. We agreed he should go for counselling and I put him in contact with a psychologist.

# How I did this research

I wanted to understand the youth as subjects responding to, and acting against, a brutal and unjust social system. To do this, I felt I had to come to terms with the meanings that lay behind their everyday human interactions. I wanted to see things from their point of view – the way they experienced, interpreted and constructed their reality. The youth were able to speak for themselves about their life experiences, their understandings of the world around them and how these forged ideas about appropriate strategies for dealing with conflict and effecting change in their society.

Over a period of about eighteen months, I spent close to three days a week in Diepkloof. It was important to participate as much as possible in the life world of the young people I was trying to understand so I could learn firsthand about their responses to a particular situation.

Since these youth belonged to political youth organisations, it was necessary to understand how these organisations operated as part of a broader social movement. Who participated in these organisations, and why? In what way did the organisations assist in creating the particular identities of the participants?

The executive of the ANCYL branch encouraged me to become a member of the organisation and to attend the general meetings that took place every fortnight on a Tuesday evening. At the first meeting, I explained that while I was hoping to participate as a member of the branch, my central aim was to do research. This was discussed in a general meeting and, while some youth were sceptical, the overall feeling was that I would be welcomed into the organisation. Members warmly referred to me as 'Comrade Monique'. Being so defined, I had to adhere to the procedures and discipline of the organisation. For example, once I was part of a meeting, I was not permitted to leave until the meeting was concluded, regardless of how late it was at night, or whether I had other commitments. Meetings were conducted in Zulu. Since my own Zulu is limited, one of the youth present was assigned to translate for me when necessary.

For the first few months of the research, I tried to attend general meetings as regularly as possible. However, the meetings finished when it was dark and when key leaders in the organisation were assassinated in late 1991, I was advised by certain members that attending such meetings could be dangerous for me. They felt my presence at the meetings could bring danger to other members since it would raise suspicion among some members of the community and the police. Why was a white woman entering and leaving the township alone at such hours? In late 1991, I stopped attending meetings that were held at night.

A second arena of participation was in the family life of the youth. This was necessary since much of their lives were spent at home with their families. Many of the interviews I conducted took place in their homes and I met with other family members. This helped to develop trusting relationships with the youth and members of the community generally. I was invited to have tea, to eat meals with family members, and to attend family occasions such as weddings. In one instance, I was asked to waitress at the wedding of one youth's brother. The other waitresses were all young women from the township. It became clear that I was perceived by this particular family as one of the young women in the township and consequently my role as waitress – rather than guest – was fitting.

Other aspects of township life in which I participated involved walking around the township, going to shops, participating in group discussions and attending funerals and memorial services. These activities were not only important for my research but also ensured my safety. My face and car became common features in Diepkloof. People would wave and call me by name in various zones in which I spent a lot of time.

Without gaining trust as a friend and comrade, it would have been unlikely that the youth would have responded to questions and probing around politically sensitive and personally painful issues. The inter-relationships within the youth community, and also between the youth and their parents as well as other community residents, could only really be understood by close observation. Although participant observation is a subjective process, it allowed me to weigh up what the youth said against what I observed. I could observe how particular people responded and I gained a sense of people's perceptions of individuals in the organisations concerned and in the broader community. This allowed me to test how people represented themselves and others, as well as to find out who the key and 'reliable' informants in the community were. I was able to develop questions as they arose in the research setting and change the focus of the research when it became necessary. Finally, I was able to gain insight into the world of the comrade youth, albeit limited since I went home to a safe suburb.

Some of the information was gained through a more formal process of interviewing. I conducted thirty intensive semi-structured interviews, each averaging about three hours, with Cosas and ANCYL youth. The people I interviewed reflected the make-up of the organisations concerned. The majority were unemployed and attending school. About 20 per cent were women. There were youth from every zone in Diepkloof. Some were new to their organisations, others were seasoned activists. The respondents were initially selected by key activists in the organisations who took account of these 'categories'. While this may appear unscientific, the responses, attitudes and concerns of the youth interviewed were in no way homogeneous. Many were critical of their organisations, of fellow comrades, and even of their leadership.

The interviews were tape-recorded, something I initially thought would not be accepted. Youth respondents, however, were generally comfortable when I used a tape recorder. I always ensured that I spent significant time informally with each of the young people before I formally interviewed them. When they were concerned that information was sensitive or too personal, they would request that I stop recording. In many instances, the interview became more of a conversation as the youth were often excited to relay events and experiences to which I could respond and probe further. Most of the youth answered even the most sensitive of questions, such as: 'Have you ever necklaced anyone?' Three of the thirty were reluctant to speak of some experiences, in particular their exact involvement in activities of ungovernability.

The interviews took place in shacks in the squatter camps, in my car, in the homes of the youth, in the Diepkloof hall and, on a few occasions, in my office or my home. The interviews were often interrupted by people entering and leaving the venue and by the noise in the surrounding environment.

The aim of these interviews was to gather in-depth information about the life experiences of the youth, the meanings attributed to these experiences, and ways of responding to them. A second aim was to get factual information about the history of Diepkloof and of the organisations.

The first category of information is generally seen to be the 'appropriate stuff' that oral accounts are made of. But the second category of information, trying to rebuild history, is more controversial. This is because, as Passerini warns (1980: 4), 'oral sources are to be considered, not as factual narratives, but as forms of culture and testimonies of the changes of these forms over time'. There is generally discrepancy and inconsistency in how events are relayed. While oral accounts of history are important, Passerini believes they need to be used with some caution.

Besides, memories are selective. All tellers have their own point of view: a perspective on what happened and on the actual participants in the event. Schrager (1983) cautions that accounts of events belong to a whole narrative environment and discourse, but researchers can always look for congruencies in the different accounts that are relayed. This, he says, can occur at any level: image, plot or theme.

While being aware of the dangers and limitations of using oral sources for factual historical accounts, I felt there were no other satisfactory sources for gaining information about the history of the youth social movements in Diepkloof. There were only scant newspaper reports of events in the township, which were inadequate as a historical source. I tried to minimise inaccuracy by using 'reliable informants' or people who were generally informed about what was going on in their own group and setting. It was possible to identify these people through the participant observation process, as well as through how they were represented in the interviews. Interviewing was at times very frustrating. The young respondents did not always arrive when interviews had been set up and we would have to reschedule. This was time consuming, but not unusual in a township where events were often unexpected and organisational tasks took primacy. Many respondents were very young and had little sense of the urgency of time.

Aside from interviewing the youth who were members of the ANCYL and Cosas, I also interviewed other key informants in the community. These included two school teachers and a principal, two social workers, a journalist, two local community councillors, two 'veterans' of youth organisations in Diepkloof in the '80s, as well as the chairperson of the local civic. The last three were also important sources of historical information. They had very interesting views on the changed nature of youth organisations and even on the individual youth activists in the area.

Language was a problem I confronted during some of the interviews. The interviews were in English. Most of the youths, particularly those who had been involved politically at regional or national level where meetings were conducted in English, spoke it well. However, there were others whose English was poor. They could not articulate their views as well as they would have been able to in their home languages. There is no doubt this led to a minimising of the richness of what they expressed. It was important to be sensitive to different vocabularies, grammar and meaning. In time, I became familiar with the respondents' usage of English. From time to time I would seek clarity. One of the informants agreed to read and comment on a draft of this book. In doing so, he also indicated a few instances where he felt I had misread the content of what had been said. While I hope my interpretation of the oral texts used is accurate, I cannot give any assurance.

For the duration of my research I kept a diary in which I noted my experiences, observations, impressions and interpretations of the meetings I attended, conversations I had, and the interviews that were conducted.

# Democratising research?

I wanted the youth who made up this study to feel that they were active participants in the research process and not simply objects of observation. After all, the research was about them and about a part of their lives that was fundamental. Throughout my research in Diepkloof, I 'engaged' with the point of view of the comrade youth. I shared my interpretation of the data provided with a number of youth and asked for comments, suggestions and indeed validation. While these insights were often provided, many of my own interpretations differed from those of the youth – although key insights were shared by 'reliable informants'.

The subject matter that was provided, largely by what participants said, hence formed what Belinda Bozzoli has called 'an analysis of consciousness'. My responsibility was to create a narrative within a socio-political context, and to make use of appropriate concepts and theories as tools for understanding. While these texts and testimonies formed the starting point of the book, they had to be read with 'a critical eye and with enough knowledge of the context to make it possible to sift the gold of true evidence from the bulk of ideology, poor memory and wilful misleading that occurs' (Bozzoli 1991: 7). I am not sure this could have been done as a joint enterprise.

On a number of occasions I asked youth respondents to read sections of the work I had written up but, for the most part, this work was not commented on. Only one 'reliable informant' made a concerted effort to read and comment in detail. He provided many useful insights and pointed out mistakes in the specific history of the local organisations in Diepkloof.

Another important source of shared knowledge came from a group of regional representatives of the ANCYL. I was invited by the ANCYL national political education officer to report on my research findings at a conference where representatives were brought together. Many of the representatives were defensive about some of the concerns and problems I raised with regard to their organisations. Their defensiveness was understandable. At the time, township youth and their organisations were under constant attack from all directions. At the end of the discussion, one of the representatives from the Western Cape stood up and said: 'I know this comrade is raising very painful issues for us, but I think we should listen to what she has to say because most of it is true.'

This book is a tribute to the youth in Diepkloof in appreciation for their time, shared experiences and, most of all, their trust and confidence in me. I was deeply moved by the amount of faith and trust the youth invested in me, evident in the very sensitive nature of the information they conveyed. I was completely overwhelmed and humbled when one of the men, an ANCYL leader, began to cry when he recalled his painful experiences in detention.

This book is my chance to give something back to the comrade youth of Diepkloof who, in a variety of ways, gave me more than I had dared hope for.

# Children of the forced removals: Diepkloof and its youth

> I live in Diepkloof Extension. This little suburb, with preten-
> tious middle-class homes – swimming pools and all – is ironi-
> cally cheek by jowl with one of the most volatile townships, the
> most densely populated conurbation of identical and muddy-look-
> ing houses in Soweto. The place is called Diepkloof. (Aggrey
> Klaaste, *Frontline*, October 1985)

The youth of Diepkloof who were part of the Charterist youth movement
understood the meaning of 'hard living'. Growing up in poverty, they had
little – if any – access to life chances and mainstream institutions. Their lives
had been a series of experiences of both structural and direct violence; they
were a world apart from their peers in the protected white suburbs nearby.
This chapter explores some aspects of what it meant for the youth to grow up
and live in Diepkloof.

Diepkloof is part of Soweto, one of the eleven regions of the City of Johannesburg. The 1991 census estimated Diepkloof's population to be around
96 000 (it grew to nearly 104 000 in 1996). Diepkloof itself is sandwiched
between Johannesburg and Greater Soweto. It is bounded on one side by
Orlando East (Johannesburg's oldest township) and, on the other side, by
Noordgesig, a coloured township.

## Diepkloof's roots

Soweto's history is rooted in the efforts of white authorities to control the
urban labour force that flooded to the towns from the late 19th-century onwards. By 1895, Johannesburg's first census showed that the population of
the nine-year-old mining camp had grown to 80 000 people, half of whom
were black, and nearly all of whom were 'unskilled, illiterate male labourers
from the rural areas' (Mandy, 1984, 174). Together with coloureds and whites,
they mostly lived in a squalid area on the western side of town. In 1904, the
bubonic plague struck and the Johannesburg municipality used this as an opportunity to enforce segregation by resettling black residents in an emergency
camp, Klipspruit, sixteen kilometres south of Johannesburg. This site was
next to what would become Soweto in 1930.

In 1930, the city council bought a large tract of land south west of Johannesburg, Orlando West. Close to Klipspruit, Orlando West was intended as a model township for Africans employed and living in the urban areas. It was supposed to keep blacks far away from the city and the white urban areas. Black residents were denied freehold rights in an attempt to ensure that Africans did not become permanent residents in the urban areas. Orlando township marked the beginning of the growth of the South Western Townships, or Soweto, as we know them today.

Soweto, along with other townships in the country, was used to ensure the segregation of racial groupings. This was particularly the case from 1948 when the National Party (NP) came into power, bringing with it formal apartheid. One of the cornerstones of the apartheid project was the development and implementation of the policy of inner city 'purification'. In the 1950s, the government was determined to remove blacks from backyards and from multi-racial areas to ensure separate residential areas for different population groupings. This involved the massive resettlement of people (mostly black) to new areas of residence in accordance with the Group Areas Act. During this period, Sophiatown and the Western Native Areas had increasingly become 'multi-racial' areas as whites moving into the urban areas tended to settle to the west of the city. White residents began to demand the removal of black residents from these areas.

The anger of whites towards black residents increased with the swelling urban protests by blacks – organised mainly by the ANC and the Communist Party of South Africa (CPSA), and usually in the form of bus and tram boycotts in the Western Native Townships during the '40s and '50s. Aside from the increasing pressure from both whites and the central state to ensure strict segregation of racial groups, the city council was also compelled to do something about the Western Native Areas, which were increasingly being defined as slum areas. According to Stadler (1987), the government made use of health and slum clearance measures as a legitimation for removing black people from the inner-city slums. In 1952, the government appointed a provisional Urban Resettlement Board to oversee the removal of blacks from Sophiatown and Newclare.

Residents of these two areas were to be moved to Meadowlands, a township to be developed next to Orlando, a little closer to town. Later in the '50s, some residents from Alexandra township were to suffer a similar fate. It is here that the origins of Diepkloof lie. The forced removals from the Western Native Areas began on 10 February 1955. By 1968, the resettlement board had relocated 22 500 families and 6 500 single people to Diepkloof and Meadowlands, both of which had been built in the late '50s for the purposes of resettlement. Within ten years, Sophiatown would cease to exist. In its place, the white suburb of Triomf was developed (Mashabela, 1988). The government stopped the removal of families from Alexandra, north of Johannesburg, in 1979. Some 44 700 people were removed from the township to Thembisa on the East Rand, and to Diepkloof and Meadowlands in Soweto, between 1963 and 1966.

Given their proximity, and their histories as resettlement townships, Diepkloof and Meadowlands were administered separately from the rest of Soweto. Unlike the rest of Soweto, which was administered by the Johannesburg and Roodeport city councils, Diepkloof and Meadowlands – jointly known as Diepmeadow – were administered by the Urban Resettlement Board. The government insisted that the board should be self-financing, and as a result Diepmeadow never enjoyed the benefits of municipal subsidies allowed to other parts of Soweto (Stadler, 1987).

# Cultural and social features

The different history and administration of Diepmeadow from the rest of Soweto, meant that there were some cultural and social features that were unique to Diepkloof (and Meadowlands). Its original inhabitants – unlike the rest of Soweto – were not migrant workers seeking work in the mines or the newly developed manufacturing industry. Many were families who had been settled in the black or mixed suburbs of Johannesburg for a long time, and who in many cases had owned property there. They were, as Rule puts it, 'well established urbanites' (1993: 10).

Although private investment made some improvement in the '70s, Diepmeadow was relatively deprived compared to other areas in Soweto. A *Sowetan* journalist, Themba Molefe, told me in an interview in 1992:

> Diepkloof is not like Soweto where you find lots of facilities for the youth. Most of the time the youth of Diepkloof are on their own. If you look at deep Soweto, there are libraries, youth clubs, and so on. When I moved to Diepkloof in the '70s from deep Soweto, there was a big difference. A youth club was not heard of in Diepkloof in the early '70s.

Administrative and historical differences between Greater Soweto and Diepmeadow gave rise to a division of youth identities in the '60s and '70s. According to Glaser, Diepmeadow youth were referred to as the 'indofaya'. Some Sowetans also remember Diepkloof youth being called 'Clovers'. Soweto youth were called 'kalkoene' (turkeys). The indofaya spoke a 'tsotsi taal', a

21

gangster language based on Afrikaans. They called the youth of Soweto proper 'kalkoene' because the Zulu-based language they spoke sounded like turkeys. The two groups of youth developed subtly different styles, which each believed represented authentic urban youth culture and high fashion. The indofaya liked jazz music, while the kalkoene liked mbaxanga, an indigenous music that emerged from shebeen culture (Glaser, 1992).

The resettlement of residents into the areas of Meadowlands and Diepkloof also probably accounts for the early political inactivity of these townships in the '60s and '70s. The social isolation of the highly militant communities of Sophiatown and Alexandra, as well as the highly repressive state machinery enforced in these townships as part of the process of resettlement, silenced residents for a time.

But, this apparent quiescence was superficial. Residents and workers in Diepkloof believed that the militant tradition of Sophiatown and Alexandra was carried over to Diepkloof and was reinforced by the relative compactness of Diepkloof as a township. As Motumi, the principal of Diepkloof's Fons Luminous High School in the early '90s, commented:

> The youth of Diepkloof are very political. Maybe this comes from their parents who are from Alexandra and Sophiatown ... We are experiencing here in Diepkloof, youth who think more of politics than of education. This is maybe because of Diepkloof's geographical position. Diepkloof is one community that works as an entity. Unlike in other areas, in Diepkloof one boy can move and cover all the schools in an hour. Schools are very close to one another and this gives rise to some form of unity.

A prominent civic activist in Diepkloof (and Johannesburg mayor from 1995 to 2000), Isaac Mogase, commented:

> If you look at the people of Diepkloof, most of them come from Alexandra township and the ANC was very strong in Alexandra township. So, most of the people who came here had ties with the ANC and they passed this tradition on. The civic in Diepkloof took up its first campaign around problems with Putco bus company and of course you remember the famous bus boycotts from Alexandra so long ago ...

Gangs were also a common feature of Sophiatown and Alexandra. This subcultural formation appears to have been transported to the 'new townships'.

In fact, gang warfare continued to be a feature of township life in Diepkloof in the '80s and early '90s, as Chapters 4 and 5 will show.

## Housing and family life

In mid-1993, Diepkloof's roads were almost all tarred and were always filled with people walking around and children playing. Women, chatting in the streets and on the pavements, have always been a feature of Diepkloof. The youth took to the streets too, particularly as unemployment increased and became more institutionalised from the mid-'70s. Informal businesses on every street corner sold fruit, vegetables, meat and chickens. At the bus terminus adjoining the police station, a marketplace evolved where men and women sold a number of wares, including 'skop' (boiled sheep's head).

Across the road from one of Diepkloof's most dilapidated high schools, Bopa Senatla, was a large open space or park. Here school-going youth spent a lot of time. Here too, a large tombstone was erected in memory of Vuyani Mabaxa in November 1992.

No matter where you enter Diepkloof, you are immediately struck by the variety of residents. Driving in through the north entrance, you see the large suburban houses that constitute Diepkloof Extension, the wealthy area of the township. Close by are the overcrowded four-roomed houses that make up most of Diepkloof's residential space. If you drive through the south entrance – directly across the road from Baragwanath (Chris Hani) hospital, the first thing you see is the Diepkloof hostel. Across the road are the four-roomed dwellings of Diepkloof's Zone 6, where one of Soweto's first shopping centres – and Diepkloof's single formal business establishment – was developed in 1975.

The township contains very stark class distinctions, easily discernable by the housing. Roughly speaking, the division is between the working and professional classes, the housed and squatter, the 'settled' and the 'migrants'. Most Diepkloof homes are the 'Prototype 51/6' matchbox houses. Forty square metres, they were mostly built in the late '50s and '60s resettlement era, when black people were removed from Sophiatown, Newclare and Alexandra and dumped in Meadowlands and Diepkloof. While richer people placed in Diepkloof Extension were allowed to buy houses, those who came from Alexandra and were dumped in Meadowlands and Diepkloof were not allowed to (Lebelo, 1988: 95). This led to tensions of 'class identity'. Says Lebelo: 'Sophiatown residents believed that the tenants from Alexandra were less clean and littered. This only began to diminish after a fairly long period of time.'

For many of the youth I met and interviewed, family life was also difficult and sometimes dysfunctional. None of the youth I interviewed for this book lived in Diepkloof Extension, the posh part of Diepkloof. They generally came from poor working-class families and, in some cases, from what could be called the underclass. In one-fifth of cases, neither parent was employed. Mothers with jobs were domestic workers or cleaners. One was employed as a nursing assistant at Baragwanath hospital. Fathers' occupations ranged from policeman to shoe repairer to cleaner at the SPCA. Four of the youths' fathers were retrenched in the early '90s, increasing the economic hardship faced by these families.

Most parents of my respondents had completed some primary school education but, in four cases, both parents were illiterate. In another five, the mothers were illiterate. None had any tertiary education. One set of parents had some high school education.

*not much literacy*

Most of the youths I interviewed were born in Diepkloof and lived in matchbox houses. Each household had between three and thirteen members (on average eight). None was married, but one-fifth of the young men had children for whom they were largely unable to provide. One of the young women fell pregnant during the period of research and had to leave school.

Three of those I interviewed were born in Soweto, but lived in one of the two squatter camps in Diepkloof. One lived in Mandela Village in a shack from which he sold basic commodities. The second left home because of conflict with his parents (particularly his father) and built a shack in People's Village, which he shared with friends. The third was a young woman who lived in People's Village with her sister and sister's child. Both sisters were still at school. Their mother lived in a squatter camp in Dobsonville where she sold chicken innards for a living. Another of the youth interviewed had been deserted by his mother and father at a very early age. He had no stable home and stayed for a few days at a time at friends' homes. His grandmother had asked him to move out of her home when he couldn't find a job.

Fourteen of the thirty youth came from 'broken' homes. Most often, they lived with their mother or grandmother (or both) because their fathers had deserted the family. There was a high incidence of male domestic violence towards both women and children. This appeared to have had two effects on the consciousness of the youth, particularly males.

On the one hand, the violence distressed and appalled them. They did not believe their mothers deserved to be 'punished'. In a few cases, they lost respect for their mothers whom they perceived as powerless in their relationships. But, in most cases, abusive behaviour of fathers led the youth to be very close to their mothers and to disrespect their fathers, whom they saw as 'bullies'. It also led, in some instances, to a desire by male youth to avenge their mothers' abuse.

*You know, when it comes to my father, I hate my father. I hate my father like I hate the policeman, ja. I have many scratches in me, many, many. Here my father hit me with a broken jug ... My father was beating my mother. I say no, no, no, now that is enough now. Beating my mother like this. Now I'm too small then but I know what you doing is wrong, I tell him. You coming from outside, you are drinking a liquor ... I say to my father he is taking a chance. He come to me with a knife. I take an electric iron and put it here to his face. Till today, I didn't see my father. (Bheki)*

On the other hand, experiences of violence in the home led to an acceptance of violence as a form of punishment and discipline, and also to a justification of violence as part of 'African tradition':

*But it's my uncles are the ones that are hitting me and rough and roughly, ja. They were breaking me, they were hitting me that time. But he do it because he love me too much, so it's a good discipline. (Senatso)*

This accords with a 1992 study on the attitudes of black children to discipline. Straker (1992) found that black children perceived strict discipline as an 'indication of concern'. Many of the young men I interviewed felt that when they had their own families, they would use violence as a form of discipline both for their wives and children:

*My parents to discipline me they beat me. When I was small I was not having any knowledge, but then up to now I could see they are putting me in the right channel of the child ... If I have a child I will beat them. I will talk to my child and if he or she never understand, then I will use the language which maybe he or she will better understand. (Chris)*

Females internalised this violence as something to be exerted against them, ~~beat~~ not by them. Most of the female youth I interviewed believed it was appropriate for their boyfriends – and later their husbands – to beat them for perceived 'wrongdoing'. They saw men as 'custodians' of women and children:

*If the guy beats the girl, they beat you with a reason ... They tell you the right thing and you, the girl, go right. They do not beat you if you go right. If you go wrong, he must beat you because he has given you a right way. (Thandi)*

Domestic violence nationally and in the townships became an issue of major concern for people in the 'helping professions'. The *Sowetan* reported on 21 December 1992 that 'two visiting British psychologists have expressed shock at the amount of violence in families and threats faced by their South African counterparts in mediating such disputes'. Diepkloof appears to have been no exception.

# Schooling and employment

The 1953 Bantu Education Act drastically affected urban townships – and South Africa at large – politically, socially and economically. This Act introduced mass education for black children for the first time in South Africa. According to Hyslop (1988), the idea of providing mass education for blacks stemmed from a desire by the state to control the thousands of youth who were idle in the townships, as well as to address the need for a semi-skilled workforce in the expanding factories. State officials, writes Hyslop, believed 'four years of schooling was sufficient to provide basic literacy skills and some knowledge of English and Afrikaans, and a basis for further education' (1988: 11). The state provided for the first four years of school, while local communities were expected to bear the costs of higher grades. The majority of schools built in Soweto and other urban townships during this time were lower primary schools. These were divided on an ethnic basis in line with the developing homeland policy, which aimed to restrict 'non-economically active' black people into ethnically divided bantustans.

The state of education for black children began to change as secondary industry increased in the '60s. There was a greater need for more skilled labour and as a result additional secondary schools for blacks were built. However, owing to the Bantu Education Act, the proportion of secondary schools as compared with primary schools remained low. For example, in 1971 there were only eight secondary schools in Soweto as compared with 44 higher primary schools. This created a catastrophic bottleneck in education (Hyslop, 1988: 458). This was addressed in 1972 as part of the state's 'reform project'. The government at the time decided to increase its spending on urban black schools and on secondary schooling in particular. While an increasing number of black students entered secondary schools, however, they remained under the control of the conservative Afrikaner bureaucrats, and schools remained vastly under-equipped, under-staffed, and geared towards the goals of apartheid governance. The legacy of Bantu Education persisted into the '90s.

There were probably about 58 600 youth under the age of 20 in Diepkloof by the early '90s, in line with more general age demographics at the time (Bundy, 1992). The community had twenty-nine primary schools and seven high schools. At a pre-school level, facilities were even scarcer. Eight mainly church-sponsored crèches serviced the entire community.

Schooling in Diepkloof was not very different from that in any other township in Soweto. Schools were administered by the 'Diep-Alex' section of the Department of Education and Training (DET). Its officials claimed Diepkloof was a difficult area to administer in terms of schooling. A Mr London told me in an interview in 1992:

> Nearly all schools in the township are not functioning properly. DET schools in Diepkloof have not functioned for a long time. Authorities failed to bring this under control. When I took over last year I was told I was getting into a difficult area ... Even at Diepdale High there is no principal, but schooling goes on.

In Diepkloof, as elsewhere, the drop-out rate of high school students was very high, particularly in Grades 9–12. According to *The Star,* the matric (Grade 12) failure rate nationally for DET students in 1992 was about 52 per cent. Teacher-pupil ratios in Diepkloof were estimated at about 1:60 in primary schools and averaged about 1:50 in high schools. General subjects such as Biology and History had ratios of up to 1:70 at high school level. Some of the schools were in a terrible condition. Classrooms at both Diepdale High and Bopa Senatla had no window panes, while the *Sowetan* reported in June 1989 that Immaculata School had been without toilet facilities for more than a month.

Most of the youth I interviewed went to school in Diepkloof. Their schooling experience was the cause of much distress. They believed the poor conditions in their schools were not conducive to learning. They felt deprived in comparison to their white counterparts:

> *Because I am black, we are not getting enough education. We are packed in a classroom and we are running short of teachers and our classrooms are having no ceiling, no windows, no nothing. Sometimes like this winter we are getting cold and that thing that the teacher is teaching you seem as if she is playing with her time because you are getting cold. Your mind is in cold, not in teaching. If maybe it is raining at night, that morning when you go to school, that class is wet, you can't understand what is happening. So that is my problem in going to school. (Thandeka)*

They were also acutely aware of the effect of the poor Bantu education system on their future life chances:

> *Personally, I don't see that we have any future as students or people, because what we learn under this education system is that we as blacks are inferior and the whites are superior. This is what we are taught. I don't see a future under such a system ...*

> *Another thing is our schools are not places for producing the future of tomorrow.*
> *Our schools are worse than prisons. (Xolile)*

Ten of the youth I interviewed had left school and were unemployed. Four had a matric and had been unable to find jobs. Two had been trying to get jobs for three years. Another three had left school in Standard 9, one in Standard 8 and two in Standard 7. Those who had left school moved in and out of poorly paid part-time jobs. Further education (specifically tertiary) was an unlikely prospect. Their families were poor, and unconnected to social networks linked to tertiary education institutions or the formal employment sector. Even though the youths I interviewed had more formal education than their parents, they were less likely to find work.

They had left school for a variety of reasons. Most common, they were failing repeatedly and had become disillusioned. Three of those who had completed Standard 9 had tried to write matric while in detention. They were never given their results and became discouraged. Another dropped out because his parents could not afford to continue sending him to school. Yet another 21-year-old youth had never attended school because his parents couldn't afford the fees. He was completely illiterate.

Violence in Diepkloof schools was a key problem for everyone connected to them – students, their families, teachers, principals and the DET. Students' complaints about corporal punishment were taken up nationally by youth organisations in the early '80s. Corporal punishment was still a vivid memory in 1993:

> *At school we were not treated as human beings … I mean if you did just a small*
> *mistake, you were beaten up and all that. So I don't think the teachers were doing*
> *justice to us and all that. (Sello)*

There were some perceived or actual links between teachers, principals and the state, which students believed led to the intimidation and arrest of activist students. Together with the use of corporal punishment, this led to students' carrying out acts of violence against teachers and principals in some of the schools:

> *The teachers would not treat us like somebody who has children. If you come to*
> *school, maybe you are hungry, you get bored and you can't learn. You start to sleep*
> *after 15 minutes. The teachers don't come and ask you what is the matter and why*
> *are you sleeping. They just apply punishment … Then also some of the teachers*
> *used to be sell-outs. The police then start to harass us. Police can take useless infor-*
> *mation from our teachers. This is when we started to beat our teachers. (Zola)*

In some cases, principals were chased out of schools and threatened with death should they return:

> *The problem at our school was that the principal had a good relationship with the security branch, because every day the security branch came to our places and they used to tell our parents what we did at school today, what we were wearing, that sort of things ... We tried to talk to the principal, but he failed to agree with us and to listen ... The principal of Bopa Senatla was chased out in 1989 or 1990, I think. The pupils chased him out because they said he was giving them problems. He wanted to avoid being killed by the students. It was better for him to leave that school. (Thabo)*

Violence against school authorities remained a major concern for teachers and principals. It led to a breakdown in the constructive relationship necessary for learning and served to deepen the crisis in education. The principal of Fons Luminous High and a teacher at Namedi High School both spoke to me about teachers being assaulted or 'victimised'.

The key source of violence and of student and community grievances in the '80s was that of the presence and activities of the security forces in the schools:

> *In 1987 and 1988, the army and police were coming in our schools. They were threatening and harassing the children, putting them in the cars and taking them to Protea interrogation room. They used to make students to point out other comrades or say they will go to jail ... Schools was nothing normal. (Senatso)*

The troops' presence in the schools made learning impossible and threatened the day-to-day activities of activists:

> *... As members of Cosas we were afraid to expose ourselves. We are afraid to have meetings and then again to just roam around the school because the police and army are walking around having guns. Then you know it was impossible to concentrate while the teacher was teaching. It was making learning to be impossible to see somebody roaming around with a gun and not knowing what he will do with that gun. (Nika)*

Police and military activity continued into the '90s. A student from Diepdale High wrote this letter to the *Sowetan* in June 1991:

> On May 29, 1991 we were all in classes and some were preparing for the half-yearly exams. The SADF and SAP came to our

school and surrounded the whole school. We couldn't concentrate and went outside. They wanted to enter the school-yard and search students during school hours.

Faced with the appalling conditions in township schools, students were obviously less than enthusiastic about receiving 'gutter education'. Despite the upgrading of schools since the '70s, the legacy of Bantu education continued into the early '90s and students continued to destroy the symbols of Bantu education. Phil Molefe of *The Star* reported on 8 June 1992 that schools were still being vandalised and damaged by students:

> 'Fons Luminous Secondary School in Diepkloof Extension, which was intended to be the pride of the black middle class living in the area, is rapidly becoming a blemish in the affluent suburb. The walls have been defaced beyond recognition with graffiti.'

But interviewees for this book claimed they were very concerned about getting an education and were aware of the importance of education for their future life chances. They were distressed about the state of the education system and their lack of educational achievement:

> *School is very important. We must know how to learn and write and to understand things. We will not be able to do many things if we do not go to school. We must be prepared to learn. Problem is that schools are very bad here in Diepkloof. (Lindi)*

Their most pressing concern was to find a job in the future. Schooling was seen as a means to getting a good job so that they could support themselves and their families. As Lumko put it:

> *If you don't go to school you are isolating yourself in such a way that you don't have access to a number of things. Life will not be good for you because you won't get a good job and all that.*

The unfortunate reality was that even those youths who were 'educated' would probably not find a job in the future. Unemployed youth were well aware of this:

> *In terms of a job you see, even though I have a matric, it's like looking for the needle in darkness. So really I think it's a question of having skills. You know, you have a matric then you fail to find a job. You end up being really tortured, going door to door and they will tell you nonsense, you see. (Sipho)*

# Leisure

There was one community hall for the 96 000 people of Diepkoof. Here weddings, funerals, feeding schemes, as well as drama and music concerts took place. There were ten soccer fields, two tennis courts, two netball courts, one public library housed in an old administrative building, one hotel and numerous shebeens.

Unemployed youth in Diepkloof, as elsewhere, were bored and frustrated. There were very few outlets for them to be creative and productive. They were sceptical of the youth clubs that had historical links to local authorities. Zola's tale is a typical one:

> *I joined this one youth club called Shining Star Youth Club. That time I was blind you see, I don't want to tell a lie. We were going on nice trips, getting food free. We didn't used to pay anything. Only to find out that it is being run by the West Rand police. It was being run by the securities. They were trying to make us to be sell-outs. So then when we realise they are selling us out ... I left the youth club.*

The more successful youth clubs in Soweto were those run by the South African Black Social Workers' Association (Sabswa) together with the National Institute for Crime Prevention and Rehabilitation of Offenders (Nicro). However, at the time of interviewing, these clubs operated only in Deep Soweto and not in Diepmeadow.

For the most part, unemployed youth interviewed spent their time relatively unproductively in the township – watching TV, listening to the radio, reading, talking with friends or being with a boyfriend or girlfriend. Many claimed they spent at least two days a week looking for a job, generally unsuccessfully. Both young men and women spent a few hours a day doing housework before they left home. Although the young women did more housework than men, the men felt a need to contribute too, especially since they could not contribute financially.

Weekends were often spent attending funerals, attending political rallies and meetings and visiting friends – very occasionally outside Soweto. Most of the young men played soccer both during the week and at weekends. Only a few of the youth I interviewed attended church over the weekends, even though their parents were regular churchgoers.

Many of the youth read mainly political material during their spare time to 'educate' themselves. Few drank or took drugs since it would have been in violation of the code of conduct of the political organisations they belonged to. The more committed spent a larger proportion of their spare time attending political meetings or carrying out 'tasks' given to them by the youth organisations to which they belonged.

School-going and employed youth had less spare time, but what little they had was spent in much the same way as that of the unemployed. They spent less time doing homework and were not very concerned about finding employment. Most of the youth were unable to escape the township during their spare time and go into town to watch a movie or eat out because they could not afford to. They tended to live in a small and enclosed – though not protected – world.

The lack of recreational facilities, together with the crisis in education and the structural unemployment, drew many youths into what Moller has called 'semi-leisure activities'. These are themselves manifestations of social, economic and political deprivation. They include, again in Moller's words, 'those activities which a young person in some cases may feel partially obliged to participate in, and when free moments available are insufficient to warrant participation in a pure leisure activity' (1991: 5). These forms of leisure differ from 'pure leisure activities', which involve both a sense of enjoyment and are freely chosen.

Most of the youths I interviewed felt a need to educate themselves informally in their spare time through reading and engaging in political discussions with other youth. Often when I met groups of comrade youth informally in the township, they discussed current affairs, such as the peace talks, the Inkathagate Scandal,◊ or even the politics of sport. 'Pure' leisure was substituted by political organisations – or, in some cases, by gangsterism.

Growing up in Diepkloof meant scant chance of finding jobs or completing school. This left the youth interviewed frustrated, angry and bored. Having no outlet to develop their potential and express their creativity, they looked for meaningful activities to fill their time and ways of changing their destinies and those of the people around them. They chose political youth organisations to give meaning, structure and hope to their lives and, in turn, they became the hope of many thousands of others in Diepkloof, Soweto and throughout the country.

◊ This was a major issue in South African politics. In the early '90s, evidence concluded that the SADF provided military training to 200 Inkatha members in the Caprivi Strip in 1986. This trained paramilitary grouping was used for a variety of covert operations, such as the assassination of leaders and supporters of the Charterist movement (Jeffery, 1997). This evidence was proof of the strong ties that Inkatha had with the apartheid state.

# 'Organise and mobilise': The emergence of youth organisations in Diepkloof

> *What is important is for a man to have discipline and to have a consistent, conscious consciousness. (Bheki)*

By the mid-'80s, townships like Diepkloof were buzzing. Meetings, both public and somewhat clandestine, were happening on every corner. Crowds of people marched in protest against poor service delivery, the collapse of schooling and the detention of activists. Barricades set up mainly by the youth were burning on the streets. And, visible everywhere, were the security forces. The second state of emergency was declared in June 1986 and lasted for one year.

Those youth who were adherents to the Freedom Charter were, for the most part, those mobilising and those targeted by the security forces. This chapter examines a segment of the Charterist youth movement as it developed in Diepkloof through the '80s. In particular, it looks at the two key youth organisations at the time: the Congress of South African Students (Cosas) and the Soweto Youth Congress (Soyco).

Cosas was launched nationally in 1979, largely as a response to the crisis in the schools. It catered for school-going youth. The formation of Cosas was very significant; it was the first organisation to adopt the Freedom Charter since the banning of the ANC in the '60s. This signified a move away from the ideology of black consciousness to that of the ANC's political programme of non-racialism. In 1983, Cosas became the biggest affiliate of the United Democratic Front (UDF). The UDF was formed in August 1983 as an umbrella and co-ordinating body of all organisations opposed to apartheid that identified with the Congress tradition. According to Lodge, 'the UDF inspired an insurrectionary movement that was without precedent in its combative militancy, in the burden it imposed upon government resources, and in the degree to which it internalised hostility toward apartheid' (1991: 29). Soyco was formed in 1982 and organised throughout Soweto. It was one of the many youth congresses that began to mushroom throughout the country in the '80s. The majority of these youth congresses, though not all, were also affiliated to the UDF. In 1987, the South African Youth Congress (Sayco) was launched as a national federal structure of the youth congresses. Sayco subsequently became the largest affiliate of the UDF, and was viewed by many as forwarding the liberation movement in South Africa.

This chapter looks at the formation of these two organisations at the local level in Diepkloof. It looks at the difficulties that were confronted by the local youth activists, and how these organisations related to the broader social movement of which they were a part.

There are several difficulties in writing on resistance in South Africa in the '80s. Owing to the repressive conditions at the time, it was very difficult for researchers to gain access to grassroot-level activists. Because of press restrictions, there is very little evidence of the processes and events that occurred in local areas. This made research in the early '90s on an area like Diepkloof reliant on the memories of people who were around at the time. As Marks and Trapido suggest, this is not unproblematic:

> It is usually believed that contemporary historians have an advantage in gaining access to recent memory of participants. Nevertheless, the oral record is constrained and shaped by the imperatives of the movement. This is not a dilemma which can be safely evaded by their successors: later historians will have to confront equally partial versions of the past constructed with the benefit of hindsight, and in the light of political sympathies. Yet contemporary historians have particular problems in achieving a perspective on their times and the necessary distance from their informants. In a rapidly changing and challenging era, it is difficult for even the most conscientious historian not to be caught up in the dramatic shifts in public mood from euphoria to total gloom, from unrealistic hope to unrelieved pessimism. (1992: 4)

Besides the subjectivity of memory, another limitation was that none of the youth activists in Diepkloof appeared to have kept any of the documents produced by youth organisations at the time – probably for security reasons.

# A history of resistance in the '80s

By the early '90s, Diepkloof was one of the most politically organised and volatile townships in Soweto, possibly even Gauteng. Chairperson of the Daveyton branch of Cosas in 1984, Caiphus Mothibe, told me:

> Diepkloof has been very politically active. Many of the leadership of Cosas in the '80s came from Diepkloof. Cosas had very

strong bases in this area, particularly at Madibane High School. Also, the number of youth arrested in Diepkloof was very high as compared with other areas.

But this had not always been the case. Seekings (1988) maintains that Soweto was relatively quiet after 1976. While youth leaders of the '70s in some other townships (such as the Vaal Triangle and the East Rand) actively developed youth structures in the early '80s, in Soweto generally, but even more so in Diepkloof, there seems to have been a leadership vacuum among the youth. In fact, in the early '80s, the youth of Diepkloof were not organised at all. While Cosas began to mushroom in many townships nationally, the youth of Soweto lagged behind. This was probably a combination of the resettlement of residents from Sophiatown and Alexandra in the late '50s, and the highly repressive state machinery in the new townships in the '60s and '70s.

This did not mean that Soweto was completely politically inactive during this period. Resistance politics did begin to take hold in the '70s in Greater Soweto. The high-profile Committee of Ten was formed in response to the inactivity of the Soweto Urban Council during 1976-77. The introduction of community councils in 1977 gave rise to further anger and discontent since they were in no way the beginnings of real local black government, as promised by the government. The growing displeasure with corrupt local councillors over a range of issues such as rent increases, evictions and shoddy service delivery, forced residents to form alternative civic organisations.

The proliferation of these progressive community organisations was 'one of the most striking features of township politics from 1979', says Seekings (1990: 145). That year, the Committee of Ten, which Chaskalson and Seekings (1988: 39) argue had 'lacked grassroots organisation and was inactive for long periods', reconstituted itself into the Soweto Civic Association.

According to its 1984 chairperson, Isaac Mogase, the first civic association in the country was in fact formed in Diepkloof in September 1979. The Diepkloof Civic Association, according to him, was formed after a collision between a Putco bus and a McPhail lorry carrying coal. Many Diepkloof residents were killed in the accident. The families did not have money for a funeral. They appealed to Mogase for help because of his previous involvement in fighting local struggles in Diepkloof. He organised a committee to raise funds for the bereaved. After the funeral, the committee continued to function under his leadership and took up other local problems and complaints.

Despite the formation of the Committee of Ten and the spate of civic organisations in both Diepkloof and Greater Soweto, some have argued that these townships were still relatively 'quiet' compared to others in the Vaal. Chaskalson and Seekings (1988) suggest four reasons for this.

First, Soweto had a more varied social structure than other townships, with residents of different classes living close together. This was not conducive to social and political cohesion. Second, incomes of Soweto residents were relatively high compared to other township dwellers. Also, the state subsidised rents in Soweto. Third, the Soweto Council was far less important in the politics of Soweto than the increasingly more corrupt and authoritarian councillors elsewhere. Fourth, the Committee of Ten was out of touch with grassroot politics and was unable to mobilise widespread support for campaigns.

Shubane argues that early support for rent boycotts was weak since reform strategies of the early '70s led to many Soweto residents owning homes and becoming 'mainly concerned with their property' (1991). He says the growth of the middle class in Soweto led to the labour movement being less of a force in the township. The development of Diepkloof Extension, otherwise known as 'Prestige Park', is an example of this.

It was only in 1982 that Diepkloof youth activists started a long and hard struggle to organise youth in the area, but these initiatives only began to take real hold as late as 1984. Initially, it was the broader adult civic struggles that provided the politically active youth with an entryway to become more involved. One of the veteran youth activists of the '90s remarked that, 'In Diepkloof we had a funny situation where in the beginning the civic was more active than the youth.'

Civic struggles throughout Soweto escalated with the Black Authorities Act of 1983 whereby the state tried to decentralise township adminstration and service delivery to poorly resourced and unskilled local councillors. The anger of residents mounted as councils increased rents, evicted defaulters and demolished shacks. This was fuelled by the lack of services councillors were supposed to be rendering, as well as allegations of widespread corruption. Residents organised by the civics called on councillors to resign. When initial peaceful protests were not acknowledged or dealt with, tactics became more confrontational and eventually violent. The violence spiralled as security forces used excessive means to curb local resistance. Councillors' homes and administrative offices were attacked. In some instances, councillors themselves were targets. The *City Press* of 3 June 1984 reported: 'Four petrol bombs were hurled at the house of Diepmeadow councillor M J Khumalo early yesterday morning, causing extensive damage.' His house was firebombed again in early 1986, according to a report in the *Sowetan*. And *Business Day* on 2 February 1987 reported 'a grenade attack on the home of Diepmeadow councillor Sinah Senokoane ... which left five children and a security force member injured'.

Civics called on residents to boycott rents and later bonds. They broadened their scope to include broader social welfare issues – the Diepkloof civic began to run feeding schemes for pensioners – and later campaigns for national political change.

The rent boycotts encouraged student struggles at the time and reinvigorated the old tactic of school and class boycotts. Student and civic struggles became inter-linked. For students, conflict shifted from the schools to the streets. For civics, concerns about the schools crisis were a community issue.

Youth activist and later trade unionist, Makgane Thobejane, confirmed that youth organisations had sprung from civic activism:

> In Diepkloof, youth were not particularly active in the early '80s, particularly the student youth. It took time for proper formations of structures in Soweto generally. In Diepkloof, youth first became caught in the process of the rent boycott organised by the civic in the area. Youth activists at the time were sporadic and reactive. It was only really in 1982 that youth in Diepkloof began to start to try to organise.

In 1982, a small group of concerned 16-year-old youths started to work night and day to set up youth structures in Diepkloof. Branches of Cosas – which organised school-going youth, and of Soyco – catering for non-school-going youth, made their presence felt in Diepkloof in 1984. Soyco later became one of the 1 200 local affiliates of the national federal youth structure, Sayco.

Diepkloof's branch of Cosas began to formalise in 1984 – five years after the national launch of Cosas – when two or three school-going youths, who had been involved in civic campaigns, took responsibility for setting it up. Since Cosas catered for school-going youth only, it was felt that some structure had to be developed that catered for unemployed and working youth as well. Mogamotsi Mogadire, who spearheaded the youth structures in Diepkloof, explained to me the thinking at the time:

> Those of us who tried to get Cosas off the ground decided Cosas activists should work with school youth, but also try to set up a youth congress to cater for youth who were not schooling. We found ourselves playing a dual role. We were student activists during the day, and in the afternoons and evenings we were active with other youth in the civic.

The Diepkloof branch of Soyco was established one year after its launch in greater Soweto. The establishment of this local branch was in line with a national Cosas resolution. 'Setting up the youth congress in the area was not easy,' Mogadire continued. 'Firstly, youth organisations were new in our area and secondly, those youth who were involved were more involved in Cosas.'

The 1984 launch of both Cosas and Soyco branches in Diepkloof coincided with the period in which resistance took hold nationally. Tom Lodge (1991a) suggests various factors that underpinned this new upsurge.

In 1983 the state, faced with an unprecedented level of foreign debt, froze consumer subsidies. This led to further financial burdens on the poor, for example, rent hikes. Drought in this period increased the cost of food production. The state's reform strategy in the late '70s led to 'weakening constraint' over organised opposition. Tension between residents and councillors grew; passive resistance became active protest. The tactic of school boycotts, which began in Atteridgeville and Cradock in early 1984, spread to other parts of the country. Students who were boycotting classes were now free to take up oppositional activities and form the backbone of community struggles. Township residents, more than ever, were ready to show their opposition to the state and its military machinery.

Finally, the formation of the UDF in 1983 was, in Lodge's words:

> a turning point in the shift of balance between the South African government and black opposition. It inspired an insurrectionary movement that was without precedent in its combative militancy, in the burden it imposed upon government resources and in the degree to which it internalised hostility toward apartheid. (1991a: 29).

Inspired by these factors, the Diepkloof branches of both Cosas and Soyco began to take up not only campaigns that had specific resonance for youth, such as the call for recreational facilities and anti-drug crusades, but also local civic campaigns and national campaigns calling for the release of political prisoners. Cosas was engaged primarily in campaigns of immediate concern to school-going youth, such as those against the age limits for school students, demands for democratic Student Representative Councils (SRCs) and an end to corporal punishment.

The number of youth participating in these campaigns grew. Youth activists paid a heavy price. In September 1984, the entire Diepkloof Cosas executive was detained. One of the executive members was shot dead by the police. The detentions sparked off another period of resistance from township youth as they called for the release of their leaders. The absence of leaders meant this campaign was poorly co-ordinated. After the leaders were released in February 1985, activities became more structured.

During 1985 the organisations set up a systematic approach to training activists. The first 'layer' of leaders undertook to train a second 'layer'. More experienced national and regional activists from the Charterist movement held training workshops at all levels of their organisations – local, regional and national. Emerging youth leaders were provided with, and encouraged to read, material about the history, strategy and tactics of the liberation movement. This often included banned material published by the ANC and the SACP, brought into the country through the underground movement and distributed clandestinely.

The second tier of leadership came to be known by Diepkloof activists as the '1985 Detachment'. It was this layer of leadership that was to hold youth organisations in Diepkloof together when key youth leaders were detained time and again throughout the mid- and late '80s.

# Repression increases

In July 1985 the government declared a state of emergency. Cosas was banned a month later. Key youth leaders were detained again and there was a temporary lull in the youth organisations.

The period 1985 to 1988 was marked by state attempts to crush organisations that were seen by the state to be core to the national uprising. The state of emergency brought with it sharp increases in detentions, arrests and the number of deaths of township residents engaged in confrontational politics. The youth, in particular, were ruthlessly dealt with. *The Star* of 12 July 1985 reported about the police firing without warning on Diepkloof youth, killing three. On 2 October 1985, in what police described as a 'crime prevention operation' in Soweto, army and police conducted house-to-house raids in Diepkloof Zone 1, urging pupils to go to school or face arrest:

> Zone 1 was virtually under siege, with armed police and soldiers asking for reference books from people found in the house. A roadblock was manned at Baragwanath Road, where all vehicles passing, passengers and those on foot, were thoroughly searched. Pupils and youth of school-going age had their arms stamped when allowed to go through roadblocks. (*New York Times*, 2 October 1985)

Youth activists I interviewed told me 200 youths from Diepkloof were detained in 1985. Many of them were not leaders. Diepkloof was probably more affected by this repression than other Soweto townships since it marked the division between Johannesburg and the Soweto townships.

# A change in tactics

The banning of Cosas and the state of emergency brought about new forms of organisation everywhere, along with new strategies and tactics. The ANC in exile called for 'ungovernability' and 'people's power' at its 1985 Kabwe conference. 'Ungovernability' meant that a situation should be brought about where the organs of civil government collapsed or were rendered inoperable by mass resistance and opposition (Swilling, 1988). In their place, the 'masses' were to develop their own structures of governance. The ANC's military wing, Umkhonto we Sizwe (MK), developed an unofficial slogan 'one day, one cop'. These messages were filtered into South Africa by the ANC's radio programme, Radio Freedom, and through the banned literature which was continually being brought into the country. The youth took up the call for ungovernability.

During '85 and '86, 'high levels of mobilisation were sustained and generalised, with chronic resistance through rent and consumer boycotts erupting on occasion into virtual civil war' (Seekings, 1993: 215). In Diepkloof, reports of political violence involving mainly youth became more frequent after the state of emergency was declared and the constant presence of the security forces in the township became a reality. A report in the *Sowetan* on 12 June 1985 chronicled the setting alight of four Diepkloof houses by youth from 'four well-known Soweto high schools'. From this point on until 1988, there were at least five reported accounts of grenade or bomb attacks on councillors' houses as well as accounts of youths ambushing police vehicles.

The state of emergency and the banning of Cosas both forced the organisation underground and strengthened Soyco in Diepkloof:

> In late 1985, we started to build a Cosas branch and to have our own programme of action. We also began to establish local UDF area committees. At this point we divided Diepkloof into zones and started to work in street committees. This was informed by the idea of people's power. Youth were now at the forefront of establishing these structures. (Thabo)

The banning of Cosas and the detention of key leadership never led to the organisation's collapse. In Diepkloof, when it was banned, it was renamed the Concerned Students' Body, and in Soweto, the banned Cosas came to be known as the Soweto Students' Congress (Sosco) and functioned as a semi-underground organisation. Later that year, Cosas simply defied its banning orders and continued to operate as Cosas. However, according to Namedi, 'after the state of emergency, a lot of students started to say the struggle was not what they thought it would be and started to be scared'. Only the most committed and militant youth remained formal members.

The secret manner in which these youth organisations were forced to operate meant that only trusted and experienced leaders were involved in deciding where meetings would take place and how they would be conducted:

> We had to develop sub-structures in different schools and each sub-structure would delegate two trusted people to go to general meetings where most things would be planned and evaluated ... Before meetings we would all meet at a point and then move off to a secret venue. Only about two or three people knew where the secret venue would be. (Namedi)

This seems to have been a general trend among youth organisations throughout the country during the state of emergency. There was no longer the luxury of organising openly and some of the processes of internal democracy within youth organsations were eroded and seen as an 'unaffordable luxury' (Johnson, 1989: 117). The scope for debate and discussion about campaigns and tactics was limited.

As tier upon tier of trained leadership was detained throughout 1986, new and less effective 'layers' of leadership emerged, bringing uncertain political judgement. As Makgane Thobejane put it:

> Nineteen eighty-six was a time when a lot of the cream of the crop was behind bars. Activities were taken by other layers of leadership. Problematic campaigns started to develop like the 'pass one, pass all' campaign. The real leadership became spectators since they were in prison. They could not take full control of the situation. These youth lacked vision of the whole situation and the youth struggle at large. There were also a lot of necklaces and killings of sell-outs during this time.

Despite condemnation from the ANC in exile regarding the use of the necklace – placing a rubber tyre around someone's neck, pouring petrol on it, and setting it alight – there were numerous reports of the use of this tactic during this period. Nekwevha (1992) also writes that the Cosas banning and detention of youth leaders coincided with the use of the macabre 'necklace' as a weapon by school students in the Western Cape for the first time.

# The era of the gangsters

In 1986, a group of gangsters from Orlando known as the Kabasas entered Diepkloof and started to randomly attack and often murder local activists, especially school students. This sparked off a war-like situation between the gangsters and the youth and residents of Diepkloof. Police were suspected of collusion:

> *The police, you know, made a blunder by showing themselves to be publicly siding with the gangsters. And then we realised that there was a collusion here between the police and the Kabasas. The problem with the Kabasas is that they were not only fighting comrades, they were fighting the community of Diepkloof. They were fighting everybody, you know, students, youth, unemployed. So, when something like this happens, obviously no one can say they are not involved. (Lumkile)*

The issue of self-defence became a reality. Students camped outside schools at night where they watched to see that strangers or known gang members did not enter the premises. According to Lumkile, 'people looked at progressive structures to stop the problem'. Youth leaders felt a need to protect the Diepkloof school students and to put an end to the Kabasa phenomenon. They set about developing defence mechanisms and creating 'youth detachments' which were groups of youth headed by a particular activist, who were assigned specific areas to watch over and protect. Eventually, they tracked the Kabasas down in a house in Zone 4, Diepkloof. Inside the house were a number of students who had been held hostage and severely beaten. The Diepkloof youth dealt harshly with these gangsters. As Thabo stated: 'The fight took three days and was co-ordinated in the form of a mob. Two gangsters were set alight by students on the second day.' The police were called and this time they were forced to take action against the gangsters.

Dealing with the Kabasas forced Diepkloof youth to organise themselves and to take careful and planned action. Says Isaac Mogase, 'The youth capacity became strong because they came together to defend themselves and their community.'

The emergence of gangs in this period was not unique to Diepkloof. It was happening nationally, according to Hyslop (1988). It appears that gang movements were indeed used, perhaps by elements of the police, as an attempt to destabilise more organised townships. Johnson (1989: 117) wrote:

> Bloody feuds escalated between youth organisations on the one hand and township gangs or 'vigilantes' on the other. Vigilantes also fought activists in well-known townships like Crossroads and Alexandra.

In 1988, key student leaders – of the first and second 'layer' – decided to leave school and were no longer directly involved in the school organisations. Their detention experiences had not only disrupted their schooling, but had also given rise to psychological difficulties that affected their concentration on schoolwork. Activists also feared they would be harassed by principals, teachers and security forces while at school. Some had written exams in detention for which they never received results, leading to further disillusionment with the school system. Some were unemployed on leaving school, others found jobs in the trade union movement. Vuyani Mabaxa and Makgane Thobejane, for example, became organisers for the National Education Health and Allied Workers' Union (Nehawu). A few, like Mogamotsi Mogadire, found places at the recently expanded tertiary education institutions.

The exit of experienced activists from youth and student politics left a serious gap in leadership. Members of the '1985 Detachment' seem to have taken over the leadership of youth organisations from this period onward, with serious consequences, as we will see in Chapter 6.

In late 1988 the gangster phenomenon surfaced once more. A new violent group called the Jackrollers appeared in Diepkloof. According to Mokwena, the term 'jackroll' was coined to refer to

> the forceful abduction of women in the townships by a specific gang called the Jackrollers which operated in … the Diepkloof specific area under the leadership of Jeffrey Brown … the most notable practices of the Jackrollers were rape, abduction, car theft and bank robbery. (1991: 16)

A report in the *Sowetan* of 25 July 1989 detailed the burning alive of a young person from Diepkloof outside Immaculata High School in 'ongoing battles' between Jackrollers and schoolchildren. The gang had 'already raped at least three schoolchildren from Immaculata,' wrote the *Sowetan* 'and the police have failed to act'. The Jackrollers, like the Kabasas before them, targeted politically active youth. They killed two prominent Cosas activists, Archie Makukeka and Mandla Vilikazi, during 1990. The youth mobilised against them. As was the case with the Kabasas, politically organised youth saw it as their role to defend the community of Diepkloof:

> Diepkloof became the site of many battles between the Jackrollers and the 'comrades'. Comrades organising from Fidelitas High School were organised as a counter force against the Jackrollers. In Diepkloof a 'hit squad' was formed which was led by a

> comrade known as 'Slovo' [Lumkile]. This hit squad went in
> search of the notorious gangsters. (Mokwena, 1991: 25)

A number of members of the Jackroller gang, including Jeffrey Brown, were killed in the months following the deaths of the Cosas activists.

In September 1989, Sosco 'unbanned' itself in Diepkloof. The *Sowetan* of 15 September that year reported that 1 000 school students from six high schools in the area 'met in the Diepkloof hall and declared their unbanning as part of the Mass Democratic Movement'.◊ The central concern of youth at this meeting was to reduce crime in the area, primarily with regard to gangsterism. The newly 'unbanned' Sosco resolved to set up a meeting between students, teachers and parents in Diepkloof to tackle crime in the area.

This new level of resistance and defiance was a reflection of national developments. In 1989, all organisations affiliated to the UDF undertook new acts of resistance. Organisations unbanned themselves and defied apartheid legislation. After that, resistance politics was to take on a different form with the unbanning of political organisations on 2 February 1990.

Local conditions in Diepkloof, together with the broad national mood of resistance, meant that by the late '80s Diepkloof youth were mobilised and active. The chapter to follow will explore the types of people who joined youth organisations, how they organised and strategised, and the identity of the 'comrade' which emerged during this period.

---

◊ The Mass Democratic Movement (MDM) was made up of organisations affiliated to the UDF, as well as other organisations that claimed to be actively opposed to apartheid. It was a tactical alliance of a wide-ranging group of individuals and organisations who came together around particular campaigns aimed at ending apartheid. In 1989, organisations constituting the MDM decided on a campaign to defy apartheid governance through a variety of forms of civil disobedience. In particular, this campaign aimed to challenge the Group Areas and Separate Amenities Acts. Large, 'multi-racial' groups of people, for example, would present themselves for treatment at historically white hospitals. They also demanded the use of recreational and transport services meant for 'whites only'. It was during this period that many organisations, such as the UDF, declared themselves unbanned.

# 5 Becoming a comrade

The period from 1984 to 1989 was one of enormous repression. People in townships who joined organisations during this time were aware of the severe consequences associated with their decision. They risked detention, arrests, harassment and even death. Young activists and supporters of political organisations were often the victims of the brutality used by the security forces during the two states of emergency. Joining political youth organisations meant a precarious existence: the costs were high. The youth had to believe the risks were worth taking. They believed and hoped mass political organisations could bring the apartheid state 'to its knees', and that this would fundamentally change their lives and their communities.

It is difficult to ascertain how many youth joined Cosas and Soyco during the '80s. Cosas did have membership cards in its early days, but these and other records were destroyed by the security police. Soyco never had a membership list as this would have been too dangerous for its members had it been uncovered by the security forces. According to youth who were active in the '80s, there were never fewer than 100 youth present at any general meeting held by either Cosas or Soyco. Old Cosas activists from Diepkloof insist that almost half the youth who attended these meetings were female but it would appear the number of females in Soyco was substantially lower. Cosas was unable to maintain a high level of actual participation by female students. Males were usually the ones entrusted with important political tasks.

> *The problem was that we tended to leave women out. We tended to focus on men to do the organising. This was our big weakness. This is why we have a problem today of not having women in the leadership. (Namedi)*

Most township youth who joined political organisations in the '80s were at school, and many of the leaders of these organisations were still at school. This was a nation-wide phenomenon, says Naidoo (1992: 146). Schools provided a base for common experiences and also a geographical space for meeting and organising:

> In the '80s, it was mostly students being involved in youth politics and also some unemployed because they had nothing to do but hang around. Working youth were a problem because the

trade unions were very weak. Workers saw the youth as sayonyo-
vas – trouble makers. (Makgane Thobejane)

Cosas had a broader vision than its demands related to schooling. It was the
first organisation since those banned in the '60s to adopt the ANC's Freedom
Charter as its guiding document. This represented a definite break with the
Black Consciousness Movement of the '70s. The Freedom Charter stressed
non-racialism as a guiding principle, and it 'provided youth with a clear set of
ideals and an all-embracing philosophy' (Carter, 1991: 207).

Schooling conditions in Diepkloof and other townships in the '80s were very
poor. Those youth who supported Cosas believed it could bring about changes.
Joining Cosas was a way of having one's demands represented and of being part
of a mass organisation that seemed to be effecting change in the schools:

> *I became involved in 1986. Then I was at school, in Standard 9. I found that within
> our school, we lacked everything – teachers, facilities... I was motivated to be part
> and parcel of the organisation in order to challenge the DET to see our education at
> our schools is inferior. That is why I became involved in politics. Even within our
> schools we had no windows in our classrooms, we shared one desk between the three
> of us. (Xolile)*

Cosas began to call for the development of Students' Representative Councils
(SRCs) which would be elected democratically by students. These SRCs would
replace the unrepresentative prefect system. Prefect bodies were appointed by
teachers and principals and were seen primarily as enforcing law and order in
the schools:

> *When I started high school, there were these things of prefects. When we came late
> to school, they close the gates. When we try to explain to the prefect why I was late,
> they don't understand. He take me to the principal. They took, what do you call it,
> stick to punish me. Then I was going to class. Then Cosas started this thing of SRC
> where people must be elected. I see now that if I am going to have a problem, I tell
> SRC. They go tell the principal and come back and tell us about it. That's when I
> see SRC is doing a good thing for students, I start to be involved with politics. (Senatso)*

Many of the '80s activist youth had been victims of severe racism through the
'70s and '80s, and had experienced incidents of racism which for them were
both extremely painful and intolerable:

> *One time it was 1982. I was 16. I came from my village to stay here in Johannes-
> burg. My father was staying in Sydenham, near Orange Grove. Well, I don't know*

> *what happened. It was raining that day. It happened when I came from the shop to where my father was staying. I have to run because it rains and the police came around and say I've stole something. I tell them I ran just because it is raining. They say no and take me to town city jail … I stay in prison about a month … And that time my schooling was messed because I could only start school in March. So I had to negotiate with the principal … And then I really came to see, no really this people are very oppressive really … That really hurt me a lot. So that's why I became conscious and feel I must do something to stop this hatred. (Sipho)*

These direct and dehumanising experiences of racism were compounded by the repressive conditions of the period. The events of 1976 were clear in the minds of the Diepkloof youth, although virtually none had been personally involved in the uprisings:

> *That thing of 1976 made me to hate white people – I am sorry to say that. So at school they explained to me what was going on and I tried to find a way of helping my people, only to find that Cosas was the only organisation available to me at the time. So I joined Cosas so I could do something to end this thing in our country … I was very proud of my political involvement because as I grew up I told myself I wanted to fight for the people. I wanted to avenge the people who had been killed. (Thabo)*

These experiences of racism, the images of the 1976 uprisings etched into their minds, and the extremely repressive conditions of the time, meant that political youth organisations became a vehicle for being heard and for effecting change. As a result, many youth were inspired to join the struggle for greater equality. The 'fight for freedom' that inspired many youth was not only meant to bring change to their lives but also to those of their families and communities.

Against this background, three broad types of members may be identified. First, there were the activist youth who felt a responsibility to join organisations. These were the 'comrades' who had a deep concern for justice and a fairly high level of political insight into the workings of the apartheid state. They felt they were on the moral high ground and were acting in good faith, as opposed to those youth who did nothing productive for themselves or the community. Namedi was one of these youth:

> *I felt I cannot go being alone when there are a lot of people suffering and not knowing what to do. I did not feel happy when I walked around here and see that people are doing nothing, just smoking and drinking. Then I came across the comrades.*

51

> *Then I felt that these are people I can associate myself with because they are doing a good thing and not just sitting around. (Namedi)*

Second, there were those who entered political organisations with no real sense of what political activism involved and a superficial political understanding. They wanted change and were prepared to make great sacrifices to get it.

Third, there were the elements whose concern was not solely the achievement of political justice. They were more interested in the personal gains they could make from joining political organisations. The 'comtsotsis' made a limited bid for existence in the '80s. 'Comtsotsis' used, in Straker's words, 'the pretext of political activism as a justification for delinquent or criminal activity' (1992: 35):

> *If we are talking of the comrades, even the comrades themselves they differed from one another. So even our comrades some few they misinterpreted the situation. Others they maybe don't want to go back to school, then those are the comrades that are misusing the name of the struggle. Even those things happen in other countries because it is caused by the tsotsis. Those things used to happen, but we try our best to make people to understand the right thing. (Thabo)*

The repressive conditions of the '80s brought with them an intense concern among young activists with the need for careful planning and co-ordination, and with ensuring the safety of members of youth political organisations. Membership was tight and the comtsotsi phenomenon within these organisations was limited during this period, but would become a real problem as the '80s drew to a close.

The existence of the three groups identified meant that at various points in time, members of organisations had different understandings of circumstances and of what responses would be appropriate.

## Strategies and tactics

Youth political organisations of the '80s have often been described in polemical terms. Seekings (1993) argues they have been stereotyped. On the one hand they are the 'Young Lions' – well co-ordinated with a highly politicised and organised membership. This is the image portrayed by the ANC publication *Sechaba*, as well as publications and speeches by youth organisations such as Sayco.

On the other hand, they are portrayed as what Seekings calls 'youth as apocalypse' – militant youth engaging in spontaneous and poorly conceived campaigns. 'This view is not only widespread – in the media, for example – but is also present, running through the history of urban struggles in South Africa' (Seekings, 1993: 3).

The Diepkloof case study seems to indicate that both these points of view have validity, but the causes for both conceptions need to be accounted for.

In the '80s, activists engaged in resistance politics had a clearer vision than before. They wished to eradicate what they saw as the structures and backbone of apartheid. The 'enemy' was clearly defined. It consisted of the apartheid state and its apparatus, as well as capitalist oppression. This clarity of vision can in part be attributed to the August 1983 launch of the UDF. Its aims, published in the September 1986 issue of *Isizwe* were to 'remove all racial oppression; ... to remove the grip of the monopoly companies over our country; to build democratic majority rule in a unified South Africa'.

There is some debate about the precise relationship between the UDF and local organisations. The immediate impetus for the UDF's formation came from the government's constitutional proposals. An additional impetus, Seekings believes, lay in the 'search for improved co-ordination between the growing number of newly formed or revived extra-state organisations' (1992: 94). Both Seekings and Swilling have given several ways in which they think the UDF influenced politics in the townships in the Pretoria-Witwatersrand-Vereeniging (PWV) region. These include co-ordinating and initiating campaigns at the township level; co-ordinating organisations at that level, and inspiring the formation of new organisations; providing a framework for activists to 'network'; and providing a national political and ideological centre.

Swilling (1988: 94) argues that the UDF had particularly strong and well-organised local affiliates 'in most areas surrounding Johannesburg/Pretoria (e.g. Soweto, Tembisa, Mamelodi and parts of Lenasia)'. Added to this, Johnson argues that the UDF's approach drew young blacks because of 'the weight of the ANC tradition and the obvious vitality of UDF-affiliated youth groups in their own areas' (1989: 110).

In Diepkloof, the UDF's impact was significant. The Diepkloof youth took up campaigns that were developed regionally and nationally, such as the rent boycott. Through the UDF, youth structures met similar structures from further afield. Diepkloof also set up its own UDF area committees to co-ordinate the activities of the various organisations in the township and developed their own generally well-conceived and planned programmes of action. Mogamotsi Mogadire told me:

> In 1986 we had a situation where we had to build a strong
> Soyco branch and to have our own programme of action and

at the same time to establish a local UDF area committee. This is when we decided to establish zonal committees and to work with street committees. This was informed by the idea of 'people's power'. The youth were at the forefront of establishing these structures. This we thought would be a more efficient way of organising.

Activist youth also tried to address what they saw as negative behaviour by the community. They called on the state to provide more recreational activities, and simultaneously they called on the youth to stop participating in self-destructive activities. Two of the major campaigns of the Diepkloof youth congress in 1986 and 1987 were anti-drug and anti-crime campaigns, aimed mainly at unemployed youth. The youth activists set themselves up as exemplary members of their community. A code of conduct adopted by both Cosas and Soyco forbade drug and alcohol abuse, as well as acts that might harm the community. These acts were considered 'criminal' by the organisations.

Diepkloof's youth organisations reflected the split in the broader liberation movement between general community activities and aims specific to young people. The youth saw themselves as part of a community that needed to work together to be an effective and unified force. They threw themselves whole-heartedly into civic campaigns and, in turn, engaged adults in the community in problems facing the youth, such as the crisis in education. This spirit of working together built up positive relationships between adults and the youth in the community. The youth realised that for the campaigns to be taken up, they needed broad support. Lodge attributes much of the success of local civic campaigns, including the rent boycott, to the 'exceptional' degree of youth activism in Soweto during the states of emergency (1991b: 95).

Because the youth felt their parents were suffering the same oppression as they were, they took time to win over adults and to develop constructive relationships. For example, when Cosas was fighting for better school conditions, they also tried to win teachers over to their side

> ... some teachers used to think we wanted to disrupt the classes ... that we didn't want to learn. Sometimes there would be confrontation between the students and the teachers, but we student leaders used to try to make sure that didn't happen. We used to sit down with the teacher and explain and apologise on behalf of the students who were disruptive. (Thabo)

The youth and older activists did not always see eye to eye, and building these positive relationships sometimes proved difficult. Aims were sometimes different. There was conflict on how to achieve particular goals. The youth often 'felt forced' to take more militant action, particularly in the light of the state's constant attempts to silence them:

> *We tried to build unity between students and teachers and parents. School boycotts became our weapon as students, because sometimes when we demanded textbooks and so on from the government, they just ignored us. Therefore we had to take action, and we used to boycott school or classes ... During those times we were looking down the barrel of a gun. For example, the same time as I was in a classroom, a soldier would be passing the window. It was bad, therefore we needed to do something as students, to change to make the soldiers stay outside the school premises. We had to make strategies, and the school and class boycotts were the strategy we had at the time. Sometimes the teachers and our parents did not always support these strategies. (Sipho)*

The truth is that some of the adults in the community were appalled at youth tactics to ensure the success of campaigns such as the consumer boycott of white-owned shops. The dramatic beginning of this campaign in Diepkloof was carried on 18 August 1985 by *City Press* which reported how

> ... groups of youths stopped cars and searched residents entering the township ... The youth seized parcels with groceries from shoppers before reminding them the boycott was on. Some of the purchases were taken and strewn on the ground with residents helplessly looking on while other parcels were confiscated.

The youth also had their own bones of contention with the adults. They felt that while adults condemned their activities, they relied on the youth to sort out various community dilemmas, particularly those related to crime. The youth were also very disparaging of those civic members who believed the youth should not be part of the civics and that there were specific issues that should be taken up only by the adults in the civics and not by the youth.

# Internal processes of youth organisations

Youth organisations were not merely trying to 'bring the government to its knees'. They also aimed to create concrete ways of organising the youth, rather than simply mobilising them. It was not good enough to simply have youth supporting the activities of these organisations. This was particularly so during the state of emergency.

The youth began to think more strategically about their role in resistance. The slogan, 'From mobilisation to organisation', became popular between 1986 and 1988. There was a concerted attempt to stop activities from being spontaneous and undirected. Youth activists stressed organisational discipline and tried to give members a common understanding of political processes and appropriate forms of collective action. This involved instilling a sense of commitment and accountability to the national liberation struggle generally, and to the policies and codes of conduct of youth organisations specifically. Being a youth activist meant attending and participating in meetings regularly, as well as carrying out and reporting back on delegated tasks. Youth organisations became sites of rigorous political education and training. As Lumkile explained:

*We would always start meetings with education. We would discuss democracy and how to organise. We would discuss informal and formal repression. Then people would understand.*

Political education was not limited to Gauteng. Nekhwevha (1992: 15) has explained how Western Cape students boycotting schools

> ... were expected to attend awareness programmes, which involved watching videos and holding workshops where discussions about the South African liberation struggle, and how it compared with struggles in China, USSR, Mozambique and Zimbabwe, for instance, took place.

Marxist texts, alternative and banned literature all formed part of the derived ideas that informed the consciousness and discourse of the comrade youth in Diepkloof, as elsewhere. The youth felt they had to be knowledgeable about what was happening around them in order to plan appropriate strategies and tactics if they were to be effectively involved in 'struggle'. Education processes and the distribution of literature became the mechanisms through which youth activists could engage in debates and discussions with members of contesting organisations and community members whom the youth hoped to 'baptise' into the Charterist movement.

Many of the youth joined youth organisations, partly in order to be educated about 'what was going on':

*Firstly when I started to join the organisation, I wasn't having that light of what this organisation was fighting maybe for ... Then I started attending meetings with*

> *them. Then it was when I started to see the light because there were political speeches being delivered in the meetings and we had discussions ... Then the leaders they told me since you are here and you are a member of the organisation, you are in the struggle and fighting for your rights and you must know that when fighting for your rights, you must know you are going to go to jail or even be killed ... This is when I started to search for more information to see what is happening in the country generally. Then by attending meetings then I became motivated and knowing what was happening and understanding myself what was the cause of me being in the organisation and struggling. (Nika)*

Youth activists were receptive audiences, wanting to imbibe and assimilate as much information as possible pertaining to their lives and 'struggle'. Leaders such as Vuyani Mabaxa became the 'organic intellectuals' who were also able to make sense of common life experiences in developing more coherent forms of understanding and interpreting the world of the comrade youth.

As repression increased during the '80s, youth organisations were forced to be more rigorous in their organising. Membership took on a whole new meaning. It was no longer good enough for township youth to simply participate in street battles and attend mass meetings to be fully fledged members of organisations such as Cosas and Soyco. They had to show discipline, commitment, and political sass (Johnson, 1989).

## Leadership and discipline in youth organisations

The need for clear political programmes and the dangerous conditions under which activists carried out their activities called for exceptional leaders. The leadership had to be respected, well versed in local and national politics and, above all, show a remarkable commitment to the national liberation movement. Youth activists knew they were engaged in dangerous activities. Leaders of the '80s were people whom the youth activists trusted with their lives. As Namedi said:

> *The '80s leadership was determined, committed, loyal and disciplined. Conditions made leadership to be determined in the '80s. To be a leader in the '80s, you had to prove yourself as someone who had knowledge and could be trusted.*

If leaders had to be disciplined, so too did members. Attempts to reduce spontaneous action led youth organisations to demand that their members behave in a 'disciplined' manner, both when engaged as members of organisations and as members of the community. Without this notion of discipline, and during a period of ungovernability, activist youth would not have had any right to recall. Organisations had the right to ask members to account for their behaviour and to reprimand members whose behaviour was deemed problematic. 'Discipline' formed a part of the discourse of activist youth. The notion of discipline is one that seems to have been central to what it meant to be a respected member of a youth organisation. In fact, 'discipline' is what separated 'good comrades' from other township youth. Members of the youth organisations were dealt with severely if they transgressed the code of conduct of their organisation, or decisions that were taken in meetings. To act in an unacceptable manner was tantamount to bringing the organisation – and consequently the liberation struggle, which the youth held sacred – into disrepute

> ... if I was to steal or do something to hurt the community, say to be doing gangster activity, I would be violating the constitution of the organisation. Even in the '80s when the gangsters were a lot, the comrades used to try to behave decent in a disciplined manner because we care about our community and our organisation. (Chris)

Youth activists believed any transgression of the code of conduct of the organisation should initially be reasoned with. Ill-disciplined youth would be spoken to and given a warning. If 'bad behaviour' was repeated, the youth could be expelled from organisations or punished physically. Discipline was crucial since irresponsible behaviour in the '80s could have had very serious consequences for its members:

> Discipline was important in times of, what can I say, crisis. Knowing what is good and right, having a fair relationship with the people concerned in the area. You should not be involving yourself in the actions that will end up compromising your comrades and your morals and conscience. Discipline means to develop your consciousness. What is important is for a man to have discipline and to have a consistent conscious consciousness. If you are disciplined then you can respond properly to things around you. If you are not disciplined there is nothing you can do. (Bheki)

Members of youth organisations in the '80s believed one had to be constantly aware of one's behaviour and not act in ways that would offend either the organisation to which one belonged, or the community in which one lived. This awareness and morality had to be 'consistent'. It had to be unfailing, capable of operating on a day-to-day basis. This state of mind and being were key to what being a 'comrade' was all about.

# The identity of the 'comrade'

It was really in the '80s that the notion of what it meant to be a comrade was developed. The term 'comrade' was broader than that of 'activist'. Whereas being an activist meant being a full-time, well-trained and competent member of an organisation, the term 'comrade' was far broader. Some have argued that it was 'a generic, ill-defined term, it came to be used to refer to practically any black youngster engaged in resistance. The term was commonly used in both the student and youth congresses, whose members addressed each other as "comrade" by which they meant "friend in the struggle" (Johnson, 1989: 140).'

However, in Diepkloof (and no doubt elsewhere) the term 'comrade' also embodied a particular morality. To be a comrade, one had to have a concern for the community and to uphold all that is 'good' against all that is 'evil':

> The comrades are different from other youth in that they are politically conscious, their approach to things is different from that youth which is not politically conscious, which is not having political education. I mean their approach generally is different like most of the comrades are not drinking and are not taking liquor and all that because they are having an education about it, they are conscious about the effect of that ... I think that comrades are the people who are disciplined, they are conscious of a number of things. (Musi)

Being a comrade meant distinguishing oneself from other members of the community. It meant being discerning in one's behaviour at all times. Drinking and taking drugs (both serious problems among township youth) were taboo. Such behaviour, it was believed, led to a lack of control over one's conduct and reduced the capacity for acting in a constructive and purposive manner.

The comrades developed their own sub-culture involving a certain asceticism, an avoidance of frivolous activities. Instead of going to shebeens and parties, the comrades would read, have political discussions and go to meetings. Most weekends were taken up attending funerals, usually of fellow comrades. These were arenas for bringing people together and popularising the national democratic movement in the '80s:

> I attend meetings every Monday, Tuesday, Thursday and Friday. On Wednesday I don't attend any meetings unless they call an urgent meeting, then I attend the meeting. On the weekends I only attend funerals if there are any ... Otherwise we sit together maybe discuss some issues ... Other youth in the township they are not

> *the same. Others they are going to the shebeens, they are spending their time there if they are free, especially on Friday, Saturday, Sunday. (Thandeka)*

The meaning attached to being a comrade led to an extension of the use of the term 'discipline'. It was also used as a verb, 'to discipline'. When a comrade acted in an 'undisciplined' manner, he or she could expect to be disciplined – with some form of punishment. Discipline could range from being simply spoken to, to being expelled, beaten or even killed. (I'll return to this theme in a later chapter.)

Discipline was also extended to those members of the community who were not members of any organisation. Community members who were seen to be engaging in activities that were deemed detrimental to the community could face 'disciplinary' action from the comrades, who saw themselves as the 'moral defenders' of the community:

> *Well, the youth of Diepkloof, I supported them to kill a gangster. They are bad boys and those people they were silly because of when our grandmothers and grandfathers go to get money for their pension, those people they just take their money and rape their grandmothers. Those things they are harassing the community and so comrade youth of Diepkloof doesn't like those things. So we need to teach those people a lesson – discipline them one way or another. (Thami)*

The fact that organised youth perceived themselves to be 'correct' and 'moral' gave them a sense that they should teach 'misguided' members of the community 'the right way'. This form of discipline generally applied to those deemed as rapists, murderers without political motivation, 'sell-outs' and, of course, gangsters. Seeing themselves as 'crime busters' arose partly from the fact that police were mistrusted and perceived as the 'enemy of the people' rather than the protectors of the community.

# Limitations and constraints

It would be too simple to see Diepkloof's youth organisations as groups of well-organised, disciplined youth with clear programmes of action and committed leadership. The organisations faced two major problems that affected their capacity to carry out campaigns in the most orderly and co-ordinated manner possible.

First, key youth leadership spent long spells in detention. Second, when the youth organisations took their campaigns and actions 'to the street', youths who were not disciplined members of organisations would join the campaigns, which introduced the risk of bringing well-meant and well-conceived campaigns into disrepute. These two problems often went hand-in-hand.

The issue of leadership moving in and out of youth organisations (as they went into and came out of detention) appears to have caused significant problems in Diepkloof. Core youth leadership could guide the youth because they were so in touch with the issues of the day. As activists, their entire existence was dedicated to the liberation movement. They were concerned that the comrade youth should set an example as truly 'patriotic' citizens so that the liberation movement would be seen as a preferable alternative. Within the community, they made every effort to form positive and constructive relationships with community members. They commanded respect.

When leaders went into hiding or were detained, new and less experienced activists assumed leadership roles. This often led to misguided campaigns, diminished control over the membership and a decrease in support from the community. An example is the 1987 'pass one, pass all' campaign, which was taken up when the majority of key leadership was in detention. This campaign was viewed as problematic by teachers and parents. They did not believe that students had an automatic right to be condoned (passed) to a higher standard at school. This campaign seemed to have manipulated the meaning of 'unity' by calling for all students to be passed (to the next grade), regardless of their capabilities and commitment to schooling. A more serious consequence was an increase in the level of political violence, to be discussed in Chapter 7.

The core youth leaders did try to develop other youth leaders who could take over in times of crisis. The practice of training a second and third layer of youth leadership was very successful in Diepkloof. A few members of the '1985 Detachment' escaped long periods in detention and were able to exert some control and leadership during periods when most of the leadership were detained. There was never a complete vacuum. As Namedi explained:

> Diepkloof youth organisations tried to deal with the problems of repression by always having at least twenty executive members at any given time so as to prevent all the leadership being detained at any one time.

And, even when most of the core leaders were detained, the youth organisations still managed to develop structures and leadership. Says Makgane Thobejane:

> There were basic problems of people seeing themselves as leadership without necessary training and experience. These were problems of personality, but they were quite easy to deal with

because most of the youth activists, the comrades more broadly,
were disciplined and accountable.

The problem of non-organised youth (as well as less disciplined members of
the organisations) participating in the campaigns of youth organisations seems
to have been an area of concern for the Diepkloof youth activists. In the '80s,
activists were only a percentage of the youth who participated in mass-based
campaigns called by the youth organisations. The other youth included both
potential members, 'hangers-on' and, in Hyslop's words, 'lumpen elements'
(1998: 198). Lodge has identified this as a problem within the UDF more
broadly. He states that 'its capacity for marshalling disciplined support [was]
questionable' (1987: 1), not unexpected with any mass social movement.

Most youth in Diepkloof were actively engaged in the street politics of the
day, even if they were not members of political organisations. The youth not
bound to a code of conduct were obviously more difficult to bring to recall
than activist youth:

> The youth leadership during this period was generally in control
> of the youth in the township. If the community felt some action
> taken was irresponsible and problematic, the leadership would
> track that person/people involved down and punish them. Lead-
> ership always knew what was going on and by what kind of
> youth. This sense of control made the people very resentful of
> youth activists and they wanted youth activists removed.
> (Makgane Thobejane)

It seems there was an omnipresence of youth activists in Diepkloof who
watched over the activities of all youth. While unaccountable youth did tend
to take the 'law of politics' into their own hands at times, they were easily
identified by youth leaders and other activists, and brought to order.

In the '80s, the youth who were identified as being primarily responsible
for undisciplined behaviour were the unemployed. These youth were seen as
difficult to organise, and as making use of political campaigns for their own
benefit. An example of this is when the youth participated in a march and
looted local shops to get food and other goods to survive. These problematic
tactics often spread to other youth who seemed to get carried away with the
process of ungovernability:

> *It was mainly the unemployed youth who got involved in things like looting. Loot-
> ing gave them something to do and would give them something to eat. Unemployed*

*youth also encouraged school youth to leave school. At times even organised youth were involved in these actions that the community complained about. The general mood of ungovernability led to this. We would discourage youth from stoning buses, for example, as this would antagonise parents. But, it was difficult to have control over youth with regards to these activities. After activities like a march anything could happen. When leadership were around, we had some control. But most youth were mobilised, not organised. (Lumkile)*

The problems and difficulties that youth organisations confronted in the '80s, such as the movement in and out of the youth leadership and the predicament of controlling ill-disciplined and unorganised youth, followed youth organisations into the early '90s. As the next chapter will show, these problems intensified following the unbanning of the ANC and other political organisations in February 1990.

# African National Congress
# Youth League
## DIEPKLOOF BRANCH

## ZONE 6

# SUB-BRANCH LAUNCH

*Now is the time for us as the youth of Zone 6 (under 35yrs) to contribute to the building of the Youth League in our area. It is important for us to attend this launch. It is high time that we made our feelings known by joining the Youth League.*

*It should be clear that we need sports grounds. We need parks, cinemas and halls. All we demand is our right o play as young people. Wre demand jobs, security and comfort. All we want is to work We need to defend ourselves as we can no longer afford losing young people. All we want is protection. Our homes must be safe.*

*Councillors must stop cutting water and electricity supplies at any time they like.*

### NGEKE SIYIMELE LENYAKANYAKA.

### Where:
**T.S. Mpanza Primary School**
### When:
**29th June 1991 at 1 o'clock**

### SEKUFIKE LAPHO SIKHATHALA KHONA!
### GO TLA NKGA GO SA BOLA!

Issued by the Diepkloof Zone 6 Interim Sub-structure (ANCYL)

# CHAPTER 6

# 'There is nothing left for the youth': Youth organisations in the early '90s

> *When Mandela came out of jail he didn't even thank us. He just seemed to think we only want violence. (Bheki)*

The material conditions of the youth in Diepkloof worsened in the early '90s. Living conditions were overcrowded – an average of eight people living in each of the tiny four-roomed matchbox houses meant Diepkloof residents had no privacy, and squatter camps were growing by the day. Riordan (1992) estimated unemployment among the economically active population nationally to be as high as 40 per cent, so the youth in Diepkloof had scant chance of finding work. Public services remained appalling, with neglected tarred roads full of potholes, burst water pipes and uncollected garbage adding to the unbearable conditions already created by the dust and smog of the township.

The crisis in education deepened and pupil-teacher violence increased. In early 1993, schools came to a virtual standstill for more than three weeks in response to a call by Cosas for a go-slow over examination fees and a strike called by the South African Democratic Teachers' Union (Sadtu) over poor salaries and the retrenchment of fellow teachers.

While these factors undoubtedly played a part in shaping the consciousness and organisation of the youth, the most crucial feature of the early '90s was the immense change in the political terrain. The unbanning of the ANC and other political organisations on 2 February 1990 ushered in a new political era of negotiations for a political settlement in South Africa.

While in the '80s the ANC was central to the resistance movement, there was a significant shift in its strategies and tactics after the unbannings. At its 1990 Consultative Conference in December 1990, the ANC committed itself to expanding 'mass action' and to consultation with local branches. John Saul (1991) points out that this did not prove to be a central focus in its subsequent strategy. Instead, the ANC focused its energies on negotiations for a political settlement at the national level. When it turned out, as it frequently did, that the state was negotiating 'in bad faith', there was anger and disillusionment not just from ANC national executive members, but on the ground among ordinary ANC members too. Frene Ginwala, who became the first Speaker of Parliament in a democratic South Africa in 1994, wrote in her capacity as head of research for the ANC:

> Having begun with the perception that the National Party was led by a man of integrity and was genuinely seeking a negotiated solution, the feeling grew that in fact the levers of state power were being manipulated in order to weaken the ANC and hence to force it in whatever negotiations followed to make compromises over the types of changes we believed were necessary in any political dispensation. There was considerable anger at the grassroots and within the ANC leadership. (1992: 9)

The ANC was determined to keep the negotiations on track. By June 1993, the NP and ANC were talking about a 'government of national unity' – a concept that preoccupied the ANC almost entirely. *The Star* of 18 October 1992 quoted the then ANC PWV region chairperson, Tokyo Sexwale, at the region's annual general meeting:

> The ANC has become a negotiations department of a struggle which concerns itself mainly, or only, with the issues pertaining to the demand for an interim government, the constituent assembly and elections.

Sexwale's words echoed the complaints of local branches of the ANC that the movement's regional and national structures were increasingly 'failing to consult'.

Novel and more sinister forms of political violence emerged in the early '90s. Whole squatter communities were massacred and many black commuters were killed on trains. Violence took on an ethnic and inter-political dimension, a factor that had been less overt in the '80s, apart from in KwaZulu-Natal. A Community Agency for Social Enquiry (Case) report in March 1992 implicated Inkatha as well as the state's secret organisations and maverick ex-policemen in the majority of these attacks. This political violence led not only to intermittent relapses in negotiations but also to local organisations having to develop defensive strategies and an inevitable weakening of the internal mechanisms of these organisations.

# A brief history of youth organisations from February 1990 to October 1993

I have already described how Sosco in Diepkloof 'unbanned' itself in August 1989.

A factor that gave local organisations impetus was the war with gangs such as the Jackrollers in the late '80s and early '90s. In 1990, violence between the Jackrollers and Diepkloof residents intensified. A *New Nation* report on 6 September 1990 stated that, in June 1990, violence between this gang and Diepkloof residents had left more than 14 people dead and scores more injured. But, according to Namedi, most of the Jackrollers had been 'eliminated' by the last quarter of 1990, essentially by the comrade youth. This was viewed by the comrades of Diepkloof as a victory of 'good' over 'evil'. The older community also seems to have lauded the comrades for protecting the community. One Diepkloof resident told me, 'The comrades have saved us from a terrible thing that has been worrying the community'. Once more, the comrade youth had mobilised as defenders of the community.

The news of the unbanning of political organisations in February 1990 and the promise of free political activity was received with jubilation in Diepkloof. A new space had been opened up for both the organised youth and the unorganised, yet sympathetic youth to openly express their sympathy with the liberation movement without fear of repression.

Soyco underwent fundamental changes. Sayco (of which Soyco was part) took the decision, at its annual congress held in Nelspruit in April 1990, to disband since the ANC Youth League (ANCYL) had returned from exile to South Africa. The ANCYL was relaunched in South Africa in December 1991. According to the organisational report provided at the national conference:

1. Sayco was to begin a process of phasing out its federal structure.
2. Sayco's membership was to find a home in the ANC Youth League and a process of formally establishing a mass-based Youth League was to begin immediately in conjunction with the ANC Youth Section.

A Provisional National Youth Committee was launched in Orlando, Soweto on 27 October 1990. Its role, according to the Chairperson's report from the December 1991 conference, was to 'bring in comrades from different strands; from Sayco and the ANC Youth Section, from prison, the underground and the mass democratic movement in general'. All concerned believed 'the ANCYL must be broader than the ANC Youth Section and Sayco. It must attract thousands of ordinary young people, including those who have not been members of Sayco, Sansco, Nusas or Cosas.' ◊

The organised youth of Diepkloof took the directive from the new national structure and began work to launch a local ANCYL, which happened on 24 February 1991. I was told there were 101 card-carrying members and about 200 youth who had not yet formally joined present at the launch. About 40 were female. A major proportion of the youth was school-going, despite the fact that they had their own, separate organisation, Cosas.

The first interim executive of the ANCYL Diepkloof branch had 12 members. Of these, four were '80s youth leaders from the '1985 Detachment', but most were new to leadership roles though not necessarily to the politics of 'struggle'. Both the chairperson and the publicity officer had a deep understanding of youth politics and of Diepkloof township more generally. This new organisation in a changed political environment also opened the way for the greater participation of women in leadership positions. Three were elected to the provisional executive. One participated until the formal launch of the ANCYL in Diepkloof. She was not re-elected. A second disengaged herself from the organisation shortly after her election, without giving reasons. The third, who was initially elected as treasurer, was moved into the role of vice-chair after the formal launch. This 'reshuffling' occurred after serious discussions within the branch.

Both men and women members believed it would be destructive for women to try to organise separately. As one respondent said, the profile of female activists should be raised so 'women can prove themselves as equal to male comrades'. This was despite the fact that there was a long tradition of women organising themselves separately in the ANC, via the ANC Women's League. One of the women argued that separate structures for women were wrong because women 'wanted to be more like boy comrades'. Diepkloof stuck to its decision, even after the 1991 ANCYL national conference urged its branches to develop separate women's structures.

In 1993, the proportion of ANCYL women members of the Diepkloof branch was probably less than 20 per cent, while in Cosas it was a little higher. A few male activists encouraged and facilitated women's participation in ANCYL, despite a general sexist attitude among men:

---

◊ Cited in *Mayibuye*, July 1990. The South African National Students Congress (Sansco) and the National Union of South African Students (Nusas) were the two student organisations affiliated to the UDF, which operated at a tertiary education level. Sansco organised black students on campuses, while Nusas organised white students. The two organisations worked very closely in a principled alliance. They merged in 1991 to form one non-racial student body, the South African Students Congress (Sasco).

*Women are not concerned about involvement or their rights. They just want to study gossip. They are highly ignorant. You find very few women reading newspaper, few, few, few ... Even when women do have a women's department in their organisations, they just talk about their boyfriends and then they fight there. (Sipho)*

Women were generally perceived as lazy and concerned with frivolous activities only. When I asked whether the role young women were expected to play in the home might prevent their participating in youth organisations, one male activist disparagingly responded this could not be seen as a good reason because 'women participate in other things like dancing and drama groups'. There was little sense among male activists that the structure and nature of the youth organisations might be a deterrent to women. Young women often said they felt shy to speak in front of so many men. They were not able to attend meetings as regularly as their male counterparts since they were expected to help with household chores. Also, their parents did not like them to come home late at night.

Cosas continued to take up more clearly defined – though poorly planned and executed – school-based struggles in Diepkloof. The newly formed ANCYL differed from the old Soyco branch in that it never developed a clear programme of action. Campaigns tended to be 'reactive' and unreflective. For example, when the municipality decided to increase rents in mid-1991, the ANCYL immediately campaigned for a renewed rent boycott, without debating the appropriateness of this or searching for other possible alternatives.

The primary focus of the ANCYL branch, like the ANC more generally, was to embark on an organising drive to secure as many members as possible. This was hardly surprising given that Peter Mokaba, then leader of the national ANCYL, stated in a report presented to the organisation's national conference in December 1991 that 'the fundamental litmus test of our own work and progress is how many youth we manage to bring under the guidance of the ANC'.

But without a clear programme of action, the branch found it difficult to maintain or develop a consistent membership base. While many youth joined the Diepkloof branch with initial enthusiasm, it waned as the quality of the branch leadership declined. Most general meetings consisted of about 30 youth only. With short-term campaigns and events it was different – politically active youth still participated in these. A combined ANCYL and Cosas memorial service and march for Vuyani Mabaxa in October 1992 drew more than 500 young Diepkloof participants.

Cosas, unlike the ANCYL, did not change its name or structure. School students in Diepkloof continued to heed calls by Cosas for school boycotts.

There were several of these after February 1990, in response to issues such as the detention of fellow students, high matric failure rates and matric examination fees. Cosas continued to have influence over school-going youth, but others in the community became increasingly critical of its tactics. During early 1993, Cosas branches in Diepkloof – as elsewhere in Soweto – came under fire from their regional leadership, as well as from the South African Democratic Teachers' Union (Sadtu) which accused them of taking up poorly conceived campaigns and making unnecessary use of school and class boycotts. It was often unclear exactly which youth were calling for various campaigns and whether they were representative of their organisations. Within both organisations there were notable changes in social base, leadership capacity, and forms of mobilisation.

# Youth joining, youth leaving

As the '80s drew to a close, it seemed that a strong and massively supported youth movement was to be a feature of the South African landscape for a long time to come. Johnson, based on his assessment of youth resistance in the '80s, presented some rather optimistic predictions for the future of youth organisations (1989: 142):

> What has developed in South Africa is a children's crusade of sorts, and the question to be asked is not whether it will continue, but in what form, and to what effect. Leaders of the myriad of youth organisations have proved their capacity to achieve unity, act democratically, devise imaginative structures in response to changing conditions, and above all, to make sacrifices. They have shown their willingness to develop their own political awareness and recognise the seniority of other components of resistance, particularly the trade unions. I believe they will proceed, haltingly, towards a position of prominence in the resistance movement equal to that of 1984-86, but as much more manageable and mature groupings – and hence they will be more effective in the pursuance of their declared aims.

Sadly, a very different picture of the Charterist youth movement emerged in the early '90s. After the unbanning of political organisations and the launch of the provisional ANCYL structures, there was great interest among the youth in Diepkloof in joining the new structure and the now 'legal' Cosas. Many Soyco members thought it logical to take up membership in the new youth organisation. For example, Lumkile stated:

> *I joined ANCYL because I used to be participating under Sayco and then Sayco was phased out then there were no alternative but to join ANCYL and to build up youth organisations again.*

The membership of both Cosas and the ANCYL remained very young, with only three working youth active in the Diepkloof branch of the ANCYL. After attending my first ANCYL meeting, I wrote the following extract in my research diary:

> *24 June 1991.* The meeting was made up of about forty youth. It was clear to me that very few of the youth present were over the age of sixteen or so. In fact, I was shocked to see that some of the youth present seemed no older than about eleven.

There were a number of reasons for this surge of interest. First, free political activity was now possible. Participation no longer meant the risk of detention, arrest, harassment and death. As Namedi said: 'I think that more youth have joined because repression is no more high and all that. They don't feel so afraid like they used to.'

Second, the 'new wave' was concerned with bringing about justice. These organisations were still perceived by the majority of Diepkloof youth as morally outstanding. Sipho explained to me why participating in the ANCYL made sense to him:

> *The organisation is trying to build the youth in terms of demands of youth and in terms of building the community. Also, the organisation discourages the youth from drugs and drinking and show them the situation we are facing and how to overcome it. So, that determination to do something good for the masses, that is what my participation is for.*

For many, the ANC was romantically conceived as a great force for liberation – a heritage of its early popularisation (something the youth congresses were renowned for doing in the '80s).

Third, some of the 'new wave' joined because they 'thought they would gain popularity and status', according to Namedi. Many experienced activists were sceptical of the 'new wave', who were inexperienced and politically naïve. The old guard believed the 'new wave' had joined for the wrong reasons which, in turn, could lead to decreased organisational control and discipline. Experienced activist youth expressed concern that there was no longer a large pool of politically astute activists who could give and take direction in a 'disciplined' manner:

> The new youth who have joined still need to be taught about struggle and how to make conscious decisions. However, serious comrades are in the minority. There are many youth who have membership cards and no understanding. (Namedi)

Fourth, youth still at school joined organisations in the hope of improving schooling conditions. Cosas, particularly, continued to provide hope for students:

> I joined Cosas in July 1991. I have to join Cosas to demand windows at school and to repair school and demand many books. I joined Cosas so I will have a history that I was fighting for people at school. Those that don't go to meetings have many problems they cannot solve. (Themba)

Fifth, the assassination of Vuyani Mabaxa was the local incident that provided a considerable impetus for youth. His murder was seen as part of a security force attempt to 'eliminate' key leadership youth in Diepkloof.

Vuyani had been centrally involved in youth organisations since 1984. He was viewed by the community as an 'authentic comrade' who was truly concerned with democracy and building strong, well-functioning organisations in Diepkloof. He was also one of the few youth activists who had a full-time job, and thus was a role model for other young people in the township. His death came as a shock to the Diepkloof community and was seen as a major loss to both the youth organisations and to the community at large.

If Vuyani was assassinated by the security forces, this is a prime example of the unintended consequences of repression. The youth who lived near his home, although not previously politically active, had seen the work he had done in the community. They were appalled by his death. All they could do about it was to contribute to 'Vuyani's struggle' by participating in the organisations that he had largely been responsible for building:

> I joined Cosas last year after comrade Vuyani died. I joined Cosas because I then see how black people are suffering. I didn't join before because I didn't understand about organisation and I was scared. But then when Vuyani died I say no man, but this is a problem – I am going to join organisation … Vuyani stayed in my street. I never talk to him to say hello, hello. (Thandi)

The fact that Vuyani was killed at a time when peaceful negotiations were supposedly taking place angered the Diepkloof youth deeply. As Lindi declared: 'I joined the organisation after the death of comrade Vuyani because the police have killed him like a dog and I knew he was a very good comrade.'

Finally, the Diepkloof youth were also aware that within youth organisations in the '80s there had been a strong emphasis on discipline and education. Even those youth who didn't join in the '80s were aware of the 'benefits' of being part of a political organisation. After the unbannings, they felt more able to be a part of the 'comrade sub-culture' to learn from seasoned activists. As Nika said:

> *In fact the ANCYL, I joined the organisation because it is fighting for the unity of all youth in South Africa and then again it prepares each and every youth to be educated and it encourages youth that they should discipline themselves all the time.*

But while many new youth were joining organisations, a large percentage of older youth activists dropped out. These included some of the key '80s leaders, including those from the '1985 Detachment'. Many felt they no longer had a clear role in struggle with the suspension of armed struggle and 'people's war'. More importantly, they perceived the process of negotiations as being the prerogative of leaders at a national level, with little regard for members of political organisations that were locally based. Mogamotsi Mogadire told me:

> The unbanning of the ANC and its approach to armed struggle and the lack of consultation, alienated old activists. Activists became demoralised. These people had been committed to a seizure of power. The transition to the ANC had an effect on activists trained in a particular political climate.

Some felt the ANC had not acknowledged the role politically active township youth had played in the '80s. Others, who had put their lives at risk for the liberation movement, felt a need to take care of themselves now and to take a break from activism.

The negotiations process left many more experienced politicised youths uncertain about how to contribute to political change. Ashwell Zwane, a member of the Alexandra Youth Congress since the early '80s, asked me:

> What is the role of the youth now? Even the ANC Youth League at a national level has not defined a role for us. What do we do in terms of Codesa? If we come together at meetings, it is to do what? The role of the youth has changed because we were in the

forefront before and now this has changed and we are in the back seat. Since the 1991 conference nothing has been done to address this problem. It was a death conference.

Other youth felt they had no role to play in the politics of the 'new era' and would simply observe from the sidelines. Commented Mogamotsi Mogadire, 'It's a sad moment to see activists we know saying the only thing they can do is vote.'

In the '80s, because of the dangerous conditions under which youth organised, there had been tight control over membership. Leaders were vigilant and activist youth were politically informed, seen as trustworthy and prepared to take up organisational tasks. However, in the 'new era', youth who were neither 'known' nor politically literate joined youth organisations:

> In the '80s, people were known and were performing tasks. Now the rate of activists is decreasing. Leaders don't know the members anymore. This causes a problem of people not being properly organised. Now people need to be educated properly and this is not happening. This is the responsibility of leadership who are not playing their role. (Thami)

Many youth did remain concerned with acting in a 'comradely' manner and doing 'the right thing', even if they lacked political and organisational know-how. They were less of a danger than another group that seemed to be on the increase – the comtsotsis – who were involved in unambiguously criminal activities, or in random 'political' activities of a dubious nature.

The ANCYL at a national level identified the increasing numbers of comtsotsis as a serious problem in many townships. In Phola Park on the East Rand, the comtsotis seemed to have taken over ANC structures, causing havoc and fear among residents of the squatter camp. Criminals masquerading as activists were taking over power from legitimate political leadership by force. A report in *The Weekly Mail* of 10 April 1992 stated: '... 16 heavily armed men hijacked a community meeting and ejected committee members from their office at gunpoint claiming to be militants from Umkhonto we Sizwe ...'

It was difficult to assess whether the criminal youth of the '90s were actual members of youth organisations or simply saw themselves as comrades. In Diepkloof in mid-1991, the youth in People's Village claiming to be comrades beat up residents in the squatter camp for allegedly being members of Inkatha or other 'non-ANC' political organisations. These actions were carried out with no previous discussion in youth organisations. It was often unclear to activist youth which individuals and groupings were involved in particular acts of violence:

*Some youth they just like to cause problems. Maybe ANCYL have got a rally, whatever. They will join there. When they come those people who are not attending our meeting they will do anything. They just involve to kill a police. They want only his gun. So this people are not part and parcel of the youth league, but they are youth. (Thami)*

Apart from the problem of comtsotsis was the issue of weapons. Large numbers of both activists and comtsotsis in Soweto had firearms. In Meadowlands and Killarney in Soweto, the youth were reportedly making their own guns called the 'quash' to protect the community against Inkatha attacks. The *Sowetan* of 7 May 1992 says the name 'quash' came from the sound the wooden firearms made when the bullet went off. It was difficult to estimate the extent of gun ownership in Diepkloof in the early '90s because it was not openly discussed by the youth. It appears many of the youth acquired weapons after ambushing and disarming police:

*There is a big problem of comrades keeping guns. But this problem is a national problem, you see, because everyday comrades are disarming the police ... and they are keeping these guns for themselves. It's not like at first when things were bad you had to go to Orlando to consult with other people to give us guns. And it's true that many of these guns have been misused by our comrades, you see harassing the community with these same guns and not using them simply for defence. (Thabo)*

They also watched the houses of whites in the suburbs and stole guns when no one was home. Not every activist perceived gun ownership as problematic. One youth respondent, new to Diepkloof youth organisations, went so far as to state that some 'undisciplined' comrades with weapons could be useful:

*We agreed that Lumkile should be involved in the defence unit although he is an inconsistent member of the Youth League and the ANC, all organisations in fact. Then because he is having a car and some weapons that he can borrow some of our comrades, then that is why we insist that he sit here in the defence units ... To me this is maybe temporary. Then whilst Lumkile is there it is just because he is having weapons that the unit can use to defend the community, but if we can get the weapons tomorrow, then people like Lumkile will be forced out. (Chris)*

Guns were viewed by Chris and others as a 'resource' needed by youth organisations. This view was certainly not representative of the general membership of youth organisations, particularly not of those who supported the negotiations process.

Chris speaks of defence units in the above quote. Defence units, known as Self Defence Units (SDUs), were established in local townships in the early '90s as a result of the sinister forms of violence taking place at the time. Their creation was supported by ANC leaders such as Chris Hani, who argued that they should play a role in protecting local communities from groupings, particularly Inkatha, which were attacking township residents, as well as from the security forces. SDUs were supposed to be paramilitary in nature and members were to be trained by the military wing of the ANC, MK.◊ While key youth activists such as Vuyani Mabaxa were centrally involved in the local SDU in Diepkloof, there was confusion among Diepkloof's youth activists about who exactly belonged to the unit, and what its relationship was to political organisations like the ANC.

Gun ownership and usage was rooted in the '80s. In his opening speech at the 1985 Kabwe Conference, Oliver Tambo, ANC president during the '80s, encouraged township youth to disarm police and steal guns from white homes:

> Pretoria has carried out its murderous plans to extremes. We must now respond to the reactionary violence of the enemy with our own revolutionary violence. The weapons are there in white houses. Each white house has a gun or two hidden inside to use against us. Our mothers work in their kitchens. We work in their gardens. We must deliberately go out to look for these weapons in these houses. It is a matter of life and death to find these weapons to use against the enemy ... The lone policeman must be made a target. He must be destroyed so that we can get his weapon ... We must learn to lay ambushes for the armoured personnel carriers and police cars that patrol the locations.

Tapes of the speech were widely distributed among the Diepkloof youth both in the '80s and in the early '90s. Several youth drew on O R Tambo's speech in the early '90s as a guide for action, without accounting for the change in the strategies and ideology of the ANC at the time. Rhetoric such as that encapsulated in Tambo's speech became part of the discourse used by the youth in justifying their involvement in political violence. As Musi stated: 'The ANC used to encourage us to disarm police. These documents are still distributed – it happens at a local level.'

The youth who had used firearms in the '80s had remained silent. They could be brought to order if firearm ownership was spoken about loosely, or if

---

◊ SDUs became increasingly controversial and, by 1993, the ANC was calling for them to disband.

weapons were used 'inappropriately'. This was part and parcel of the expected 'disciplined' behaviour of youth activists at that time. The lack of leadership control in the '90s led to the loss of this discretion. On 29 May 1992 Rapu Molekane, a member of the ANCYL's national executive, was quoted in *The Weekly Mail*:

> 'In the '80s if you had a gun, you didn't tell anyone. Now it's the fashion … Whereas thugs of the past could be disciplined by organisations, those of today are armed, dangerous and untouchable.'

For some of Diepkloof's comrade youth, firearms were used for the first time with the advent of the Kabasas and later the Jackrollers. Weapons were initially obtained through members of Umkhonto we Sizwe (MK), who were operating underground in Diepkloof at the time. However, little or no training seems to have been given to these youth in Diepkloof. The youth learned to use the weapons 'in action':

> *We have this motto where you say you learn on the battlefield. You know the whole thing started with the Kabasa thing. We would go to MK soldiers we know and they would supply us with guns. They would say comrades we don't like giving you this, but comrades do you know how to use these things? Then we said no comrades, give and we will see for what, you know, then some would give us. And then when we arrived at a scene we just used it. I was never trained by someone to use a gun. I just saw myself using a gun and that was that. (Lumkile)*

Youth organisations in the early '90s had a membership that was largely new and politically naïve. They were also plagued by youth engaged in 'unsavoury' activities – problems compounded by increased gun ownership and indiscretion in the use of weapons.

## Ideological patterns

Although the ANC encouraged the youth to organise themselves into the ANCYL in the early '90s, it no longer saw the youth as the central force for change. The ANC leadership now frowned upon the strategy of ungovernability that it had forwarded in the mid-'80s. The youth were asked to support the negotiations process and to back up ANC demands with 'mass action'. For the comrade youth, this was not an easy pill to swallow.

The new mode of politics gave rise to a variety of responses in the ANCYL Diepkloof branch. Four different 'ideological' groupings emerged:

1. Youth activists, particularly the '80s 'old guard' who, although they might have disagreed with some of the ANC's decisions, felt morally bound to support the ANC and publicly did all they could to strengthen support for its decisions.
2. The 'new wave' who supported ANC decisions more uncritically.
3. A large grouping that felt angered and frustrated at the ANC decisions and strategies and stated their opinions openly.
4. Comtsotsis, who while angered at the apartheid system, were more concerned with the personal gains they could make through criminal activities than with developing any ideological orientation.

The ideological cohesion of the '80s weakened significantly in the early '90s. This perhaps reflected the lack of ideological cohesion in the ANC generally,◊ and was compounded by the lack of consultation between national, regional and local structures. Many local youth activists complained they were getting no guidance from the regional and national leadership of Cosas, the ANCYL and, of course, the ANC itself.

Much of the 'repertoire' – to use a term from Clingman (1991) – of the Charterist social movement of the '80s was carried into the '90s. Comrade and activist youth in the '80s had developed their own discourse and understandings of the world around them, as well as their own ways of responding to particular situations. The 'comrade sub-culture' in the '80s had portrayed violence as a legitimate means of bringing about change. This was attributed to the 'intransigence of the regime'. Many of the youth I interviewed in the '90s continued to make use of this rhetoric:

> *We need to make it impossible for the people who are participating in the institutions of the government to govern this country. So I mean by destroying the institutions which facilitate the government that will in a way destabilise part of the government itself and eventually we will attain what we want. (Musi)*

It is not surprising that rhetoric of this kind persisted in Diepkloof in the early '90s. Conditions in Diepkloof either remained unchanged after the unbannings or worsened. The strategies of the '80s still seemed relevant for many youth. However, the formal code of conduct of the broader ANC tradition would

---

◊ There was disagreement within the ANC leadership about the negotiations process and to what extent settlements should be made with the NP. There was also disagreement about ANC tactics, such as the use of mass action to put pressure on the government. Consequently, certain more hardline members of the ANC leadership came to be known as the 'hawks' while more conciliatory members were known as the 'doves'.

not allow for this. The early '90s were marked by disunity regarding strategies and tactics.

# Internal processes, leadership and organisational culture

I became aware of the youth's alienation when attending a general meeting of the Diepkloof Youth League on 15 September 1991. It took place within days of the signing of the Peace Accord that committed all political parties to a code of conduct for all political activity. The aim of the Peace Accord was to provide a regulatory framework to create a safe, secure and politically toler-ant environment in South Africa. The security forces were seen as central to creating this environment, and were also party to the Peace Accord. In theory, the accord should have been of major significance to the youth. However, the agenda of this meeting consisted of apologies, minutes, report from executive meeting, and general. When I got home I wrote in my research diary:

> I found the agenda very disturbing. Not only was it entirely bu-reaucratic, but it made no mention of certain current and perti-nent issues. I raised the fact that the Peace Accord was to be signed the following week and asked whether this shouldn't at least be discussed. While some members agreed it was an important issue, the overall decision taken by the meeting was that the accord was going to be signed anyway, so why bother to talk about it.

The youth felt powerless to affect broader political processes. They were ada-mant that their contributions would be disregarded by higher levels of author-ity. Many of the youth were unemployed and felt resentful towards the ANC for neglecting their needs when manyof them had given years of their lives to activism. As Namedi stated:

> *Most of the 'old' leadership are frustrated and are unemployed and the ANC has not taken care of them. They have to spend most of their time trying to get funds for themselves.*

'Finding funds for themselves' often translated into gangster activities. At least three high-profile members of the 'old guard' were accused by community members of involvement with gang activities in the early '90s, including rob-bery, rape and even murder. There were, at the time, conflicting reports from Youth League members about whether these 'old' activists were involved in 'problematic activities'. The 'old guard' felt a sense of loyalty towards their long-time comrades:

You know this problem with Lumkile [a renowned activist in Diepkloof since 1984], I don't know. In 1986 when we were in detention together, he came out and he was very strong. But when I went into detention again and he did too, I don't know what happened to him along the line but I know that people came to report that he was involved in gangster activities and I actually said go and get him and I will talk to him ... I mean some of them became drop-outs in school and nothing was done for them, you know, in terms of development or anything. Some of the youth of the '80s because of their experiences are now a lost generation. (Isaac Mogase)

The history of the chairpersons of Diepkloof's ANCYL branch also demonstrates the decrease in the calibre of youth leaders and the decline in organisational coherence. Namedi was the first chairperson of the interim executive elected in early 1991. As a member of the '1985 Detachment', he was considered to be of the same calibre as Vuyani Mabaxa. During the 'reshuffling process' later in 1991, Namedi was withdrawn as chairperson and placed in another executive position. This move, decided on by the executive and ratified by branch members, aimed at moving Namedi from a 'figurehead' role to an 'organisational' role. Thabo, the new chairperson, was arrested shortly after his appointment and charged with murdering his sister's boyfriend. Although he stated his innocence, he was subsequently implicated in other criminal activities. In December 1992, he was shot and critically wounded by police during an attempted robbery. Thabo was 'relieved' of his term of office at the 1992 annual general meeting. Sipho was elected the new chairperson. But because he had only moved to Diepkloof from the Northern Transvaal in 1990, he was at a disadvantage since he did not know the township very well.

This illustrates one of the key problems of youth leadership in the early '90s – the changed nature and capacity of youth leadership. The new leaders were perceived by past leaders as poorly trained and without the ability to organise township youth effectively:

The loss of '80s leadership has weakened the Youth League in the sense that we have a new brand of activists not grilled in Congress politics and with no sense of being grilled in strategies and tactics. They are not able to broaden its base. Seasoned activists could have helped in this regard. If we still had these activists, they could train new people along this process. There is what we call a leadership vacuum. (Makgane Thobejane)

The loss of the select youth leadership gave rise to a nostalgic longing by both the youth and adults in the township. Isaac Mogase, leader of the Diepkloof civic, was one of these people. He confided to me that:

> It is true that I am missing youth of the calibre of Vuyani and Bob Marley [Makgane Thobejane]. I have missed them a lot. I used to work with them a lot in the civic. It seems consistent leadership is not there. The new leadership are not known.

The new leadership appeared less able to give direction to the organisations, or to develop adequate programmes of action:

> *Youth don't see why they should go to meetings and be part of struggle. Leadership should be doing something on the ground and giving direction. They just go to meetings and give report-backs. Before we had programmes of action and could guide action (Namedi).*

While the 'old' leaders were well informed about political and local developments and how to organise, this appeared to be lacking among the new leaders. It led to a decrease in control over organised youth and a high drop-out rate in active membership:

> *The previous leadership was more determined, committed, loyal and disciplined in the '80s. Commitment and determination changed due to conditions. Conditions made people to be committed in the '80s. But in the '90s the ANC is doing everything and there is nothing left for the youth. (Lumko)*

The general feelings of alienation and purposelessness meant Diepkloof's youth organisations failed to develop and carry out a clear programme of action with well-organised campaigns. The ANCYL attempted to set up an anti-crime and clean-up campaign, as well as to establish co-operatives to service unemployed youth:

> *Well, in Diepkloof youth now we are trying to take up crime and such things and making youth to participate in our structures. We are trying by all means to stop the crime which is very high in Diepkloof. We need to work together in terms of the question of unemployment of which most of our youth are facing this problem. What we are doing is not enough in terms of just organising the people. (Sipho)*

None of these well-meant campaigns took off, mostly because of weak leadership:

In the '90s, youth flocked into organisations. We did not have to go out and organise. A political programme was lacking ... Some people in leadership lack a clear vision of beyond and analysis. Political education is not taken as seriously. Only a few youth involved today are committed, others have a basic understanding but lack the determination to learn and be creative. (Makgane Thobejane)

Meetings became more bureaucratic and discussion vague and undirected.

*We discuss about South Africa, you see and about this comrade died. And then you must see what these comrades did in South Africa. That is why we are sad about those comrades died. In the organisation they also tell you that you have a good future because you are in organisation. (Thandi)*

While the *content* of the youth meetings in the '90s differed vastly from that of the '80s, the actual *style* remained much the same. In all the meetings I attended, there was a concerted effort to ensure broad participation of members present. Internal democracy was taken very seriously. When contentious issues were raised, the meeting tried to reach agreement by consensus. If this was not possible, a vote by show of hands directed the meeting. There was always a great show of respect for whoever was chairing the meeting, including a woman.

The concern for discipline became more of a central theme for youth organisations in the '90s than it had been a decade earlier. Thobejane believes this happened in the absence of a political education programme. Activist youth continued to consider themselves the 'moral defenders' and protectors of the community. Sello remarked:

*I only can say the youth, especially the comrades is the only people that can defend their parents and their sisters ... The youth are the ones who are energetic and the ones who will bring a good future.*

As in the '80s, being a 'defender of the community' meant eliminating what was perceived to be evil or indefensible in the eyes of the comrades. The right to discipline was again extended beyond the membership of the youth organisations:

*The comrades are knowing the right thing. Sometimes they are giving the people who are doing the wrong thing a discipline. Maybe they sit down and talk to them. Maybe they take this person and whip him. It's good because then this person knows this thing is bad like to shoot or to rape a person. (Themba)*

Justifications for disciplining and the form the discipline would take were decided in street committees. With the decline of street committees in the '90s, there was less accountability in the issuing of 'discipline'. Some comrade youth, such as Thabo and Lumkile, were involved in activities deemed as 'thuggery' by others. This was particularly prevalent within Cosas, whose membership base was very large. Other students and teachers were easy targets for frustrated and angry school-going youth.

While it was easy to mobilise young school students around educational grievances, it was less easy to impose organisational discipline:

> Other members of Cosas, they don't have discipline, so we are there to help them, to show them the code of conduct. Others they are members of Cosas but at the same time they are thugs. They do threaten students if they don't come to meetings and make the teachers to feel they can't teach properly. (Zola)

The increased involvement of youth activists in acts of thuggery disenchanted community members, including the youth:

> These new comrades now they are not behaving in a right way like before. They are just going around hitting people for no good reason and telling people how to behave or they will beat them. So the adults are not liking these things. Even me, I am member of ANC Youth League but I will not attend meetings until these things stop to happen. (Thandeka)

Such activities gave rise to deteriorating relationships between Cosas members and school teachers. One of the youth activists told me he had failed the year. He did not believe he deserved this. He went to see the school principal, held him by his collar and demanded to be allowed to go on to a further year of study. The headmaster then told his class teacher to 'condone' him to the following year. The youth who told me the story did not believe there was any problem with his actions, although some other youth felt such behaviour was not warranted.

Commentators and residents of Diepkloof condemned the participation of school-going youth in violent activities in the early '90s. The *Sowetan* of 3 March 1992 reported that pupils from Bopa Senatla High School petrol-bombed a house they believed belonged to a policeman. Following the attack, some of the youths involved in the attack told me they weren't sure if the house owner was actually a policeman or a member of Inkatha. Later the same month, *The Star* reported that youth claiming to be Cosas members set fire to an oil tanker in Diepkloof Extension. The driver died. A youth claiming to be a leader in Diepkloof subsequently told the *Sunday Star* of 24 May 1992, 'The DET does not want to listen. Maybe if they see we mean business they will stop the exam fees.' One of the youths from the Cosas 'old guard' was particularly perturbed by the oil tanker incident:

*killing*

> *No one can condone such actions. There must be explanations. These actions that are taking place today are not well co-ordinated. People in leadership are not there when these things are happening. If youth feel there is not a response to this and that demand, they take action which is not defined. (Namedi)*

The once harmonious relationship between youth organisations and the civic went rapidly downhill. According to informants, the civic was 'always condemning' the behaviour of the youth. Similarly the youth regarded the civic as being engaged in 'sell-out' politics, particularly with regard to negotiations with the Soweto City Council and the Metropolitan Chamber in 1991. At these negotiations, the parties agreed that monthly lights and water rates would be raised by R10 every three months, growing to R95 a month by the end of the year. Diepkloof youth organisations, believing this to be unacceptable and unaffordable for their parents, threatened to organise a rent boycott. The rates negotiations were eventually broken off, an indication of both the clout that organised youth maintained in Diepkloof as well as the civic's concern to maintain or rebuild positive relations with them.

## Retaining the 'comrade identity'

Despite poor levels of organisation in 1993, the ANCYL and Cosas continued to play an important role in Diepkloof. Their capacity to reflect and determine certain themes of youth identity remained strong:

> *The comrades are not a lost generation. If we were a lost generation we wouldn't be involved in structures that are so constructive. We would be selling dagga, stealing cars ... You wouldn't care about the future. Why involve ourselves in structures that do care about the future when we don't care about the future, you see? (Lumkile)*

Being a comrade continued to mean 'doing the right thing' and being disciplined. Members of youth organisations were expected at all times to portray a positive image of their organisations. Alcohol and drugs were still frowned upon. It was considered unacceptable for activists to carry out political tasks when they were not completely sober. Members of youth organisations could be severely disciplined for contravening the code of conduct. My research diary of 8 July 1991 contains the following extract:

One of the key issues to be discussed at the meeting was that one of the executive members of one of the zones of the Youth League had come to a meeting drunk. It was clear that this was perceived as a very serious offence by the membership. What should 'happen' to this person had to be discussed. After much debate, and with some guidance from the chair [Vuyani] it was decided that the person concerned should be suspended from the executive concerned. It was my feeling that this was a fair 'judgement'.

The morality and subsequent discipline of the comrades had positive spinoffs. Vuyani, and others like him who maintained the moral high ground, were called 'authentic comrades' by some older members of the community, including social workers, teachers and even local councillors. These older community members took the view that 'authentic comrades' represented a positive alternative to gangsterism. They felt organised activist youth had a sense of responsibility and could be reasoned with. One Diepmeadow city councillor told me: 'The organisations have influence over the youth. If they could preach the Codesa gospel, the youth would go along with it.'

It is significant that this positive attitude remained in the minds of some. As Mr Tloteng, a senior social worker with Nicro in Soweto, put it:

> The older people in the community appreciate youth in organisation. They feel these youth make things change. This is different from gang youth who they see as destroying the community. The political youth try to avoid chaos because they say this is tarnishing their image.

It is unclear to what extent this positive view reflected the general feeling of the Diepkloof community, or how these perceptions might change.

While the comrade identity was retained, we have seen that the early '90s brought with them numerous changes to the nature of youth organisations that experienced increasing problems in terms of control and leadership. This changed organisational pretext had major implications for the nature of collective action, particularly collective violence that was carried out by the comrade youth. The chapter to follow explores the types of collective violence that were carried out by these youth and how these changed in the early '90s.

# 7 'We cannot die alone': Engaging in collective violence

*In Diepkloof here you have to be involved in violence. Without youth there isn't anything that can take place. The youth, every youth is in the forefront and in this time of violence, youth must be in the forefront. After that come our parents. But there is nothing going on without the youth. (Sello)*

To what extent have township youth been victims of violence? To what extent have they been agents of political violence? What types of violence did these youth engage in? How were acts of collective violence organised? Were acts of collective violence a gendered activity? This chapter, in addressing these questions, also shows how, with the decline of discipline and effective leadership within youth organisations in the early '90s, acts of collective violence became increasingly less directed and coherent.

Seekings argues that 'conservative commentaries on conflict in South Africa equate youth with violence' (1993: 5). This perspective was reinforced and encouraged by television representations of political violence in the '80s when the context of the violence was withheld from viewers. Instead, what was portrayed were scenes of 'unruly mobs' causing mayhem – burning cars and buildings and engaging in acts of murder. Crowds of protestors and demonstrators were portrayed as mindless, and as manipulated by a small core of agitators (Posel, 1990).

While such portrayals and understandings are problematic, there *was* a strong relationship between political violence and township youth. During the '80s and even the early '90s, township youth were the main recipients of state violence. But they were not simply victims, they were also agents of collective violence. In their struggle against oppression and in response to repression, township youth engaged in acts of violence as a perceived means of bringing about social justice.

In understanding political or collective violence, it is important to understand the link between violent acts of the state and those of collective actors (C Tilly, R Tilly & L Tilly, 1975: 97). Acts of collective violence carried out by politically active youth in the '80s and early '90s, I believe, should not be understood as simple 'mob rule' but rather as having a distinct rationality understood by participants. Second, they should be viewed not as discrete and indiscriminate acts, but as part of a continuum of a broad range of collective action. Third, political violence carried out by members or supporters of social movements is largely as a result of the repressive actions of the state.

While violence is often viewed as irrational and unproductive, there are those who take a different approach to the use of collective violence in political studies. Parekh (1972: 78), for example, insists that collective violence may be

> ... directed at achieving justice or at fighting a mad and suicidal policy ... It may then be the most expressive form of the most rational emotion ... Violence is generally a language through which feelings of desperation are conveyed, and therefore it has a meaning, a sense, and cannot be senseless. To treat it as senseless is to deprive the political language of a useful dialect.

While collective and political violence carried out by comrade and activist youth in Diepkloof was directed and effective in 'getting their voices heard', these acts changed as the Charterist youth movement and its organisations declined. With this decline, increasingly chaotic and perhaps less acceptable acts of collective violence emerged. Collective violence remained rational and purposive even if the purposes became more contested and controversial.

# Types of violence in which organised youth were involved

The kind of political violence that the Charterist youth movement engaged in – 'revolutionary violence' – suggests that violence was most likely directed at the state, its personnel, property and allies (McKendrick & Hoffman, 1990). In the case of the comrade youth, this conception of political violence is very narrow. The recipients of political violence carried out by the comrade youth could include anyone or anything regarded as obstacles to the goal of 'liberation'. For the youth I interviewed, gangsters, 'criminals' and 'counter-revolutionary' forces such as Inkatha were legitimate targets of collective violence.

There were four broad types of political violence perpetrated by Diepkloof youth: against direct agents of the state; against those seen as indirectly serving the state (representatives of capital and vigilantes); against 'misdirected' members or sympathisers of Charterist organisations; and against 'ordinary' people who offended the 'collective conscience' of the broader community.

# Revolutionary violence against state agents

Revolutionary violence was the most common form of political violence perpetrated by the youth in the '80s, given its link to notions of people's war. In the early '90s, this kind of violence continued, but decreased, most probably due to the ANC's condemnation of such acts of violence.

This violence, which often included killing, was carried out by youth and community members heeding the ANC's 1985 call for ungovernability. Seekings argues that during this period the ANC 'encouraged almost any form of militancy as contributing to the intensifying "people's war" against the state, in which the youth were the heroic combatants' (1993: 97). Statements by the ANC and the SACP in the '80s clearly illustrate this:

> In many current upheavals the people make heroic efforts to engage the enemy using rudimentary weapons. Street battles and barricades take shape where mass confrontation with the enemy becomes acute. At their initiative, the youth and other sectors set up Self Defence Units and combat groups. This creates the basis for the revolutionary movement to raise mass revolt to higher forms of insurrectionary action, by popularising the skills of armed combat and giving all-round leadership and direction to the popular combat formations. (SACP 1989: 54)

I have already mentioned the way in which Oliver Tambo's speech at the 1985 Kabwe Conference was circulated in the township. Tambo, in defining ungovernability, stated:

> ... the battles are raging in our country. The war of liberation continues and it is intensifying with each passing day. The time has come for us to acquire weapons to pay the minority regime back in its own coin. We cannot die alone. We cannot bury alone ... We must respond to the reactionary violence of the enemy with our own revolutionary violence.

Diepkloof youth who were part of Charterist movements took these calls to action very seriously in the '80s. In the '80s they identified 'targets'. 'Targets' primarily referred to the security forces (the police and the military). Those 'targeted' as the rightful recipients of political violence were identified by the youth as being related to anything or anyone associated with the apartheid state:

> *I feel very angry toward the police and hope that they can disappear. When I see them I feel that the car can roll over with them and die all of them because they are no good for the people ... Of course in our mind the approach of the police will never move. When we see the same uniform moving around the township – the same cars and the same uniform must not be here. The police that are inside must die. (Senatso)*

There were very strong feelings of antagonism and hatred towards the police. The police themselves were perceived as irredeemable. Because of this, they needed to 'disappear'. Their disappearance would only result with death or a completely changed police force. The very symbols of the police (their cars and uniforms) evoked negative emotions. This attempt to obstruct the police from 'moving around freely' in the township fed the legacy of ambushing police vehicles in Diepkloof through the '80s and into the early '90s. In many of these incidents, police were killed and their vehicles burned.

Similarly, the corrupt and inefficient councillors governing Soweto in the same period were also targeted and killed. These councillors were seen as 'direct agents of the state' since their job was that of carrying out 'apartheid policy'. They were responsible for rent increases and the evictions of residents and squatters, often with the assistance of the security forces:

> *Our councillors they are just state puppets. They don't talk with us, you know. They just oppress us. That's why sometimes we attack these councillors because we don't want them to be running our townships. (Zola)*

Attacks on councillors continued into the early '90s. Despite the changed political context, many youth I interviewed believed 'the overthrowment of the regime', as Zola expressed it, was still necessary. Sello stated that, 'Political violence is correct because I mean those people who are targeted are the people who are participating in the institutions of the government. Because the issue is that we should try to make it impossible for them to govern this country.'

# 'Extended revolutionary violence' against indirect state agents

Those who informed the police and the state on activists' activities and their organisations were also seen as deserving of severe punishment. Informers and vigilante forces were seen to be undermining the hegemonic project of the liberation movement. The killing of informers from the mid-'80s to the early '90s was not uncommon and has been well recorded by the Truth and

Reconciliation Commission (TRC). Perhaps the most well-known case was the gruesome killing of Maki Skosana in Duduza township in 1985. Skosana was beaten and then necklaced by a group of township residents who had accused her of being an informer.

Public violence of this sort was often explained by South African psychologists, particularly forensic psychologists, as resulting from a process of 'deindividuation'. They argued that during incidences of collective public violence, individual self-awareness and self-monitoring became diminished and 'mob psychosis' led to decreased individual responsibility (Manganyi, 1990). While such an approach tends to undermine individual conscious intentions in these situations, court case testimonies have revealed that people who took part in the public killing of informers (such as Maki Skosana) were traumatised and even shocked by their involvement (Manganyi, 1990).◊

Although according to youth interviewed, informers were killed in Diepkloof, there was more reluctance to do this than was the case with security forces in Diepkloof:

> *Ah, we will know these informers. For my side I don't like killing an informer. I beat an informer. If I finish to beat him, I take him and put him down. I talk to him. I tell him the history of the struggle. You must stop an informer. (Bheki)*

Informers were perhaps seen as more redeemable than members of the security forces. They could be reasoned with, spoken to and possibly converted.

Attacks on vehicles belonging to big businesses and well-known firms were also seen as legitimate. These vehicles represented capital, which was perceived to be upholding the state through financial assistance* and undermining tactics of the liberation movement, particularly consumer boycotts. According to Thabo, in the '80s 'even cars that delivered goods from town were our targets because they prevented our boycott, which was supposed to undermine the economy'.

A common incident in the '80s, the hijacking of Putco buses – which service township residents – was still considered justifiable in the early '90s by some of those I interviewed. This was especially the case in Diepkloof which

---

◊ One of the Duduza trialists made the following statement in court: '… I was scared to tell my mother what I had done. I went to sleep but could not sleep. I was shocked. I was shaking and had diarrhoea. I never thought I could beat Maki …' (Manganyi, 1990: 291).

* This understanding was developed in Sayco in the '80s and is reflected in its draft policy document of 1987. It states: '… in the same situation of national oppression of the black people, colonialism and imperialism facilitated the imposition of the capitalist mode of production on our soil … the black section, particularly the African working class, suffer super-exploitation and all the worst ravages of capitalism'.

does not have a railway station. Residents were therefore dependent on taxis and Putco buses for transport. It was believed that since residents gave Putco their business, they 'deserved something' in return:

> In the Youth League we have decided not to hijack any more, we will only hijack buses ... the issue of Putco it was a result of thorough discussion. If we do have a funeral, and then Putco refuse to give us buses, for the fact that he is dealing directly or indirectly with the community. People are paying money to Putco, so Putco must also help us. But we have decided not to hijack cars, only buses. (Chris)

The death of a comrade was seen to be the death of one who had sacrificed himself or herself for the 'masses'. Political funerals had become rituals reinforcing unity through the symbolic meaning of pain and sacrifice. Since 'people are paying money to Putco', it was felt that Putco should 'service' the community in return for patronage.

There continued to be 'incidents' in the early '90s. On two occasions, on driving into Diepkloof, I noticed cars burning in the middle of the road. When I asked what had happened, I was told these were probably cars belonging to 'firms' that had been attacked by school students. I was informed by Chris, however, that 'the company car is our target. Then we take the car and you may go and do whatever you think will be of benefit to you by then. But they will never kill you.'

Vehicles belonging to whites also became targets. The youth believed whites had power in South African society since, as Chris said, 'Parliament is directed to the whites.' Attacking their vehicles was a way of bringing attention to struggles being waged in the townships:

> White cars are targets. Through the whites we are having access to complain to the person in government. Then we will show the government through the whites that we don't like what the government is doing. (Chris)

In the early '90s, the Diepkloof branches of the ANCYL and Cosas identified the hijacking of vehicles as 'problematic' and 'inappropriate' in the climate of negotiations:

> We have now decided in our structures that the hijacking of vehicles must stop. There is no point in doing these things anymore since ungovernability is not our strategy anymore. But it is difficult to stop these things because some of the youth today are not disciplined. In fact, I would say that it is mainly thugs who are doing these things. (Lumkile)

The new social base of the Charterist youth movement in Diepkloof and the increased loss of control of youth organisations over their followers made the directing of new tactics very difficult.

In the early '90s, Inkatha and the hostel dwellers were defined as the key vigilante force by Diepkloof youth. They were seen to be creating violence to undermine the ANC's organisational capacity and to stall the negotiations process:

> *Inkatha is killing people. Those peoples they say they don't like boycotts and they don't want stayaways. Those people they just want to go and work because they say they respect the white man. So it's a problem again because they won't let us to get liberation. (Thami)*

Inkatha undermined the liberation movement by opposing key ANC tactics. For some youth, Inkatha had become 'the enemy' and, like the key enemy of the past – the state and its direct agents – deserved to die:

> *If Inkatha come to our area, they will rest here, all of them … If they come to Diepkloof, I don't want to lie to you, they will get died, all of them, not even one is going to be injured. They are going to get died and there's nobody to go in the hospital. They will go in the ice, government ice. (Bheki)*

Bheki very clearly saw the rightful home for Inkatha members as the state mortuary.

There were other indirect agents of the state who were identified, indicating a more sophisticated understanding of how youth defined 'the enemy'. Even teachers and principals who were perceived to be aligning themselves with the state or the DET as an institution became recipients of political violence. Vehicles of DET officials were destroyed, and teachers not clearly identified with 'progressive forces' were beaten up or chased out of schools under the threat of death should they return.

In an interview with Mr London, a DET official, I was told there had been many incidents of violence towards teachers and principals in Diepkloof high schools. In early 1992, the vice-principal of Diepdale High was chased out of the school and threatened with death by students should he return. Mr London advised the vice-principal to continue to administer his school and that 'only his physical being must not be there'. Mr London believed teachers and school buildings were easy targets for school-going youth who were angry at the DET and 'cannot go to Pretoria and speak to the minister'.

Unsympathetic teachers and principals posed a real problem since they could easily identify activists to police. Going to school became a dangerous activity for activists and this led to great resentment:

> *The youth they force out some of the teachers and principals. We are sick of going to jail. You see the police are coming to our school. They ask the teacher, do you know such and such a person? When we find that person going out of school, we find them arrested by the police. When we ask the principal, he say the state of emergency is for all students. So we can't accept such a thing and sometimes we have to beat such a teacher. (Senatso)*

# 'Mechanical discipline' within youth organisation

Recipients of violence were not restricted to those outside of the liberation movement or 'the enemy'. Violence was also enacted against those within or sympathetic to the Charterist social movement, and active in Cosas and Soyco:

> *In the organisation we are taught to use revolutionary discipline. This means that we apply discipline theoretically. Then if a person fails to act properly, we use a mechanical discipline, another method of discipline which is going to affect a person physically. (Thabo)*

'Mechanical discipline' referred to physical punishment used to bring fellow comrades and activists 'into line'. It was meted out after other forms of 'theoretical discipline', such as speaking to comrades about the 'right way' and giving them 'tasks' to carry out, had failed:

> *We don't encourage that but sometimes we are forced to use that. We tell ourselves that we are fighting for liberation of the people – each person has thousands of other people he or she must relate to. So if we feel that he or she is misusing their trust or misusing the name of the organisation or discrediting the name of the organisation, we say that mechanical discipline must be used because we are fighting for the people and not for ourselves. (Thabo)*

Failure to adhere to organisational decisions was seen as potentially leading to a loss of unity, endangering the organisation and its members, or bringing the organisation into disrepute. It was not the individual who was important in the 'struggle', but rather a larger group of people because the youth were 'fighting for the people and not for [themselves]'. As Thabo explained: 'Mostly, we ask people to do tasks, but the discipline can be more harsh, like sjambokking. But we try not to use this thing.'

Violence against a fellow comrade was seen to be a last resort for extreme cases of misconduct. The most common form of violence used against members of youth organisations was that of sjambokking or beating. No examples of more severe forms of violence, like killing, were mentioned.

For organised youth, bodily pain was a 'language' understood by all – a language absorbed, perhaps, from the authority figures both at home and at school:

> We only assault someone as a last resort. I mean if we see that we have failed completely ... I've been involved in disciplining comrades. Like during our school days, you see some other guys they were going out of class and burning cars. We'll have to talk to these guys and if doesn't work, we have to take stronger measures ... I mean sometimes sjambokking them or suspending them from the activities of the organisation. At times we even had to kick them out of the organisation. (Lumkile)

Youth leaders like Lumkile were attempting to maintain a form of perceived morality and purpose in struggle. Decisions should not be made by individuals, and actions should not be undirected. Mechanical discipline was used to assert the authority of the organisation and of the collective. The collective was of primary moral concern. It was assumed that it was a greater punishment to exile someone from the organisation than to sjambok him or her.

# 'Scrupulous violence' in the community

The comrades' sense of themselves as 'moral defenders' of the community was crucial to their sense of identity. Organised youth had a strong sense of their own behaviour as upright, with the right to monitor the behaviour of others. Structures of 'people's justice' such as 'people's courts' were formed to ensure a 'people's morality' in the light of the perceived illegitimate operations of the formal legal courts and the police.

The formation of structures of 'people's justice' was a feature of many townships in the '80s. People's courts enforced a new morality associated with liberatory projects. They were alternatives to the formal criminal justice system (Scharf & Ngcokoto, 1990). In Diepkloof, there were street committees. People's courts were not operative in this area. Street committees operated in tandem with the civic, and often paralleled the anti-crime campaigns in which the youth were very active. They exerted discipline over 'deviant' community members. This often involved violence.

There were organised youth who believed that even gangsters could be 'rehabilitated'. The anti-crime campaign in the '80s was an attempt to prevent crime through urging local government to build recreational facilities and educating the community about the divisive and destructive nature of crime:

> *With the gangsters they should be educated. I mean we should try to end that kind of situation and educate everyone not to be a potential member of the gang. You should try to quell that thing before it happens ... But if this does not work, for the sake of normalising things within the community you know, you have to speak to people in a language which they understand the most ... So if it means beating them up, that is okay. For the sake of the community and all. (Sello)*

Youth organisations presented themselves as alternative positive structures to gangs and as protectors of their communities. Many youth felt ultimately they had no choice but to become 'law enforcing' agents because of the problematic role played by the police. As Thandeka stated:

> *The comrades are involved in violence against the gangsters but if ever the law would take responsibility to arrest those people who are doing those things, there will be no more violence because they will arrest them.*

For this 'policing' work to take place effectively, it was necessary to have resources – particularly weapons:

> *The thing is dangerous. People were dead, shooting dead and injured. That was the problem with these gangsters. As a youth we are undefended. Of course the gangsters are having weapons and cars. When the gangster comes you stand with the gangster and talk what's happening. Either the gangster will come back after five minutes and shoot the youth. So this is very bad. (Themba)*

Comrade youth felt compelled to get weapons, particularly firearms to fight the gangsters, and thereby not be completely vulnerable to them. As Senatso stated: 'Then we said no, we must finish this fight. Let us arm ourselves strong and strong. We have finished the gangsters until death.'

In the early '90s, street committees had broken down but violent methods continued. Rape and murder were seen as the worst crimes that could be committed, deserving very severe punishment:

> *There was this issue where a boy raped a 17-year-old girl. Then what we did after we get information from the meeting, then we decide to go to the family and consult with them concerning this issue. Then only to find when we go inside, the family itself is not united. But they just decided maybe to undermine us. Then what we did, we just took their child and go with him outside and do what we thought is*

> *good for us ... we beat him ... We didn't want to kill him. We prefer to beat somebody. He's now in the ICU [intensive care unit] at Baragwanath. That's what we usually do ... It's not my aim to kill somebody, but if it came to the push, then I would do so. By push, I mean if they retaliated and tried to kill you, we will have to retaliate in return. (Chris)*

The first point to note here is the assumption that the families of offenders would be sympathetic to the comrades' mission and prepared to reason with them. The use of the words 'not united' indicates this was not the case in this instance and, as a result, the offender had to be taken outside and punished without the consent of the family. The second is that the youth stressed they would try to 'reason with' the offender verbally, before using more severe methods of discipline. Finally, death was not usually seen as the preferred penalty for misconduct. Death was seen to be consequential rather than intentional.

In some instances the word 'killing' was used to mean 'beating':

> *If there's a rape, you must be killed. There's no doubt if you are killing or raping because you are doing rotten things ... Not to say you just kill ... Maybe if I'm putting a word, killing is wrong. It can be a punishment that you are having a good understanding of our language. It means just to punish. That's why I'm hearing we calling it killing is wrong. Not to say we kill him, murder him. No, we are not murderers. To kill means to hit someone. If I really mean to kill, I will use the word destroy. You see, if you destroy someone, they won't be able to appear again. Isn't it? (Zola)*

Zola's use of the word 'kill', even if not literal, is very harsh and indicates the seriousness with which he views crimes such as rape, and that the punishment should be so severe as to make the offender almost invisible – unable to 'appear again'. Zola is also at pains not to debase the comrades to ordinary criminal murderers.

There were instances, however, where the intent had clearly been to kill offenders:

> *Even to discipline a person I don't like it because sometimes okay, a person maybe he do a murder and then say comrades they just take a necklace and then they hit him and they just die. Then you will run. So these things are terrible. (Thami)*

But even in cases where people were killed, sometimes by horrific means such as necklacing, youth like Thami were not comfortable. Their response was not to stay and watch, but to escape the scene of such violence.

Comrade youth generally felt the Diepkloof gangsters should die and 'not appear again'. Gangsters were seen by many as irredeemable, as existing outside of community morality:

> *Okay, well the youth of Diepkloof I will support them to kill a gangster. They are bad boys and those people they are silly because of our grandmothers and grandfathers they go to get money for pensions. Those people they just take their money and they are harassing the community. And so, youth of Diepkloof doesn't like those things so they go there and kill them because of the comrades are against that they are killing our people, so they kill them. (Thami)*

Scrupulous violence was the most common form of violence carried out by organised youth in the early '90s. This should be seen in the light of increasing levels of crime in the township, inadequate policing, and these youths' continued belief that it was their duty to protect their community. However, while their intentions may have been honourable, with decreasing levels of organisation and guidance and deteriorating relationships with the civic, these activities were deemed to be somewhat problematic by elders and even concerned comrades.

# The necklace – 'weapon of the youth'?

In any discussion of political violence in South Africa, the 'necklace' surfaces as a source of bewilderment since it is particularly gruesome and excessive. As mentioned previously, the necklace refers to 'a weapon of terror that involves placing a car tyre around the neck of a victim, filling it with petrol and setting it alight' (Cock, 1991: 227). The youth are widely perceived as the perpetrators of this form of violence. However, for those such as Straker (1992) who have done research into the attitudes of youth regarding the necklace, it is clear that a divergence of opinions regarding involvement in this activity exist.

Four of the youth I interviewed in Diepkloof claimed to have been actively involved in a necklacing. Most interviewees were not in favour of the necklace as a 'weapon of struggle'. Necklaces, where they were used, were unplanned and were not part of the strategy of Diepkloof youth organisations. One youth who had been involved in a necklacing said:

> *We don't decide in organisation to put a necklace. It's just maybe your own emotion. You must understand that if all of us were emotional ... We don't do it for fun, ja ... I don't think it's a good thing. But if someone don't want to listen, it was*

> our strategy to show that we are serious. Not to say that maybe it's our principle to put a necklace. (Jabu)

Perhaps because they lacked the legitimacy given by youth 'morality' to other forms of violence, acts of necklacing were remembered as far more traumatic incidents than any others:

> Necklaces they were used on vigilantes like the Kabasas. Well, necklacing you see it is not good. Okay, it's not good that our people are doing necklaces, but some other people they are sick. So they say, use necklace for that ... I did watch a necklace, but I feel bad you know. If you necklace a human being it's so terrible ... You just sleep badly because you think of what is happening there and you'll never eat because when you get food the food it tasted bad like it burn me. So it's a problem. (Thami)

Two of the youth told me they did not think the necklace had a positive value. Those who did, saw its 'beneficial' nature stemming from the horror of the act. It was a strong deterrent, a form of 'retributive punishment' in the Durkheimian sense:

> I don't have problems with the action of necklacing. It's an effective strategy of preventing things from happening. People who have committed grave crimes deserve necklacing. It prevents things from happening again ... I myself have witnessed a necklace. It is not a morally good thing but there is no other option. There is nothing as effective as necklacing. The ANCYL does not support these actions, these things happen locally outside of meetings. (Jabu)

Despite such views, the necklace cannot be viewed as the 'weapon of the youth'. Most organised youth strongly opposed necklacing as a form of punishment. While many youth had witnessed necklaces, very few – four only – would admit to having taken part in one. When it was discussed, it was in tones of outrage. As Namedi said:

> The necklace is terrible. I don't understand why these things should happen ... I want to believe that while the youth have been involved, it has not been our comrades that have been doing that.

# Who was involved in political violence?

Organised youth I interviewed were certainly not the only youth engaged in political violence. As noted in Appendix 1, a distinction needs to be made between social movement organisations and social movements. While people involve themselves in activities they perceive to be in line with the general interests of a social movement, they are not necessarily structurally part of any organisation that constitutes that social movement. With a social movement as large as that of the Charterist youth movement, it is difficult for organisations to have control over their own membership. In urban contexts, this is a common phenomenon. Morris suggests there 'are structural features which make the creation and maintenance of organisation within the township more difficult than within the workplace' (1990: 49). He continues that

> ... organising in a township and maintaining organisation as well as accountability of the leadership are more complex [than in the workplace]. There is a diversity of classes and class interest and the constituency is far more spread out ... The space to be organised is far more fluid, with individuals constantly moving within it ... In the urban terrain, if organisation is established, it is often difficult to maintain. A prime difficulty is to create workable, durable structures for this purpose. (Morris, 1990: 64)

For this reason, it is difficult to assess exactly which youth were involved in acts of political violence. Also, such an assessment is dependent on the often vague perceptions of youth activists themselves as to who was involved and who was not. Straker believes that in the '80s 'among the youth, it was the majority who participated in the eruptions. The youngsters who did not participate in these popular uprisings were the exception rather than the rule' (1992: 19).

While organised youth in Diepkoof tried to bring the organising and disciplining of political violence under their control (especially in the '80s), this was not always possible:

> *Most of the youth in the '80s were involved in people's war. What we learned is that most of the youth wanted violence, not just sitting in meetings and discussing. If you call a meeting they won't attend. But if there's action, maybe 20 of organised youth can go into the streets singing and it ends up more than 100. They like action. (Thabo)*

In the '80s, 'action' meant making the township ungovernable, which involved a number of acts of violence in which youth were willing to participate. In the face of high state repression and terrible material conditions, violence was in fact a means of 'having a voice heard'. Organised youth seemed unclear as to who participated in various acts of political violence and even why certain of these activities took place at all. Many of the youths were unknown to each other:

> *When we hear of taxi drivers being killed and cars being ambushed, we can say it is the comrades and the ordinary youth. Others they think their own things to a bad person. I don't know why they are doing this to the person or why this is happen like that. I don't know what is going on. (Senatso)*

It appears that in both the '80s and the '90s, youth who were not organised 'hijacked' well-planned actions of the youth organisations. Organised forums of the youth were exploited by ordinary and often criminal youth to express their own anger and anxiety, as well as for personal and material gain:

> *Okay, with the killing of policemen for example, this is what is happening. Most of them what do this come from the ANC Youth League ... they are in the forefront. Then some youth just go there to harass. Maybe ANC Youth League have got a rally, whatever. They will join there, they go together that way. When they come back with those people who are not attending they will do anything. They just get involved with killing a police and when they killing a police, they holding his gun. Generally these youth only want his gun to do a criminal thing. Then these youth are not part and parcel of the ANC Youth League, but they are youth. (Thami)*

In the '80s, youth activists – some of whom were unemployed – blamed unaccountable and problematic violence in the township on unemployed youth. The involvement of unemployed youth in such activities was to be expected since they were 'available for direct action ... somehow "desperate" ... and without responsibilities, and therefore, irresponsible and reckless' (Seekings, 1993: 68). As Mogamotsi Mogadire told me:

> It was mainly the unemployed youth who were doing such things as looting. It gave these youth something to do and also something to eat. Unemployed youth [told] school-going youth to leave schools and participate in such things not authorised by the youth organisations.

However, even in the '80s, there was also concern about 'undisciplined' school-going youth. As Lumkile said:

> *During school days, you see other guys will go and burn cars outside and we are in classes. When the police come, we are being teargassed for nothing ... You know, unplanned action you see.*

In the early '90s, school-going youth seemed to be the ones who were identified most often as being responsible for 'problematic' acts of violence. Nika told me:

> Today, the school youths are causing us a problem. They don't want to go to class. Then they simply going out of the class and hijacking cars and such things. So it's a problem.

In most reported incidents of political violence of this nature in Diepkloof in the early '90s, school students were identified as the participants. On 27 January 1991, *City Press* reported that the daughter of former mayor Jacob Matala died after his house was petrol bombed by 'rampaging pupils'. On 15 October 1991, *The Star* reported that pupils at two local schools barricaded streets and set fire to a lorry after ransacking a house in the area. These incidents followed the death of local ANCYL leader Vuyani Mabaxa. The same newspaper, on 19 February 1992, reported that a group of schoolchildren attacked a police colonel who was stuck in a traffic jam. The *Sowetan* of 5 March 1992 reported that a group of school students from Bopa Senatla bombed the house of a man they claimed was a policeman. Both *The Star* and the *Sowetan* on 20 May 1992 carried reports that Diepkloof school students had set alight an oil tanker and stoned private cars during a protest against a decision to increase school fees.

# Where were the girls and the women?

It is often assumed that male youth only were involved in political violence. Very little has been written about the role gender plays in relation to youth politics, especially youth violence. Comrades are often portrayed as militant young men whose use of violence is part of their overall sense of masculinity. Even academic definitions of the comrades negate the existence of women completely:

> The 'comrades' who call themselves 'the young lions' have been the 'shock troops' of black resistance in the last four years. Boys as young as 10 years old have been involved in violent confrontations with the SADF and the SAP. They are socialised into violence through a particularly militaristic conception of masculinity. This is reinforced by a gender-defined sense of social solidarity, a brotherhood of combatants. (Cock, 1991: 225)

Campbell states that the 'crisis in masculinity amongst African men', largely as a result of unemployment, can help explain why they engage in acts of violence' (1992: 614). These men, she argues, participate in acts of violence (political and personal) to 'compensate' and 'reassert' their masculinity, as well as to affirm their 'traditional' domination, particularly within the family, which is also in a state of crisis. For Campbell:

> Violence and masculinity are closely intertwined in the macho culture of resistance. The comrades characterise themselves as hard, ruthless and disciplined with no time to rest and no time for pleasure, as living under the constant threat of death and prepared to sacrifice their very lives for the struggle if need be. (Campbell, 1992: 624)

Men's 'social identity', to use Campbell's term, as well as the patriarchal construction of South African society, are crucial to understanding men's dominant role in resistance politics. However, the dichotomy between militant macho males and empathetic alienated females is perhaps a false one. While youth politics and organisations have been, and remain, male dominated, young women have been active too – albeit in small numbers. It is commonly believed, however, that women are subject to men's safekeeping:

> War is a gendering activity. It both uses and maintains the ideological construction of gender in the definitions of 'masculinity' and 'femininity'. Women are widely cast in the role of 'the protected' and 'the defended'; often excluded from military service and almost always ... from direct combat. (Cock, 1991: x)

For Segal, however, violence cannot be equated with masculinity. She believes that when women are placed in situations where violence is commonly used, they tend to resort to violence as do men:

> For example, women prison officers were found in the late 19th century to enforce especially severe physical and corporal punishments on their female charges ... Similar tales of women's zealous use of force, including conventionally defined acts of violence, appear in many accounts of women's behaviour when in positions of power. (Segal, 1990: 268)

While Cock's assertion that men are the protectors may be generally true of both conventional and some guerrilla armies, it needs to be challenged more significantly when looking at the actual experiences of women in 'wars' based in the community. It also seems that the role men in these situations attribute to women, and those that women attribute to themselves, can be dissimilar. In Diepkloof, I met women comrades who not only repudiated the notion of themselves as inherently more peace-loving than their male counterparts, but who wanted to be directly engaged in activities involving 'hard violence'.

Young women in Diepkloof did participate in political violence, particularly in acts of arson. Two young women told me they had recently been involved in setting fire to the home of a man believed to be an Inkatha supporter. According to them, about 20 per cent of the participants in such activities were women.

Other women comrades in Diepkloof expressed a willingness to engage in political violence and wanted to 'learn' how to do so effectively. Thandi went as far as to say that she wanted to learn how to kill someone. She went on violent 'missions' with the comrades to gain experience for the future:

> *I do go with the comrades if they are going to kill somebody. I will want to see how are they going to kill him ... Maybe next time, I will know how to hit that person.*

Another, Lindi, believed no woman could do something bad enough to deserve death:

> *But I will only kill a man. If they would kill a woman I would become scared ... To see a woman killed is a shame ... You see the women are not involved in bad things like to be an impimpi◊ or such things. So with women we mustn't kill them, we must talk to them.*

Two young women comrades felt it was acceptable (and desirable) to beat a person who was involved in misconduct, but that killing someone was not desirable:

> *I go sometimes with the comrades when they go to give someone a present [physical punishment]. But, not every day, you see. If they go to beat this guy, I am going. But if she is killing the people, then no, I am not going. I am not wanting to see the dying peoples. But when they beat someone, I just watch because I am new in the organisation and I must see how the comrades are doing something. (Thandi)*

The women comrades mostly appeared to be spectators, rather than direct participants in acts of violence. One young woman who was personally 'scared'

◊  Zulu word meaning informer or spy.

to watch acts of violence, nonetheless believed women who did so were to be admired:

> *The female comrades they are going to watch violence, you know. Not to put their hand to help, they are going just if they hear somebody has been killed or they are doing this and this. Well, you know the females are the first ones to go running to see what happened. These women are brave, but I am scared of these things. (Thandeka)*

Observing political violence was seen as an act of support for such activities. Yet despite women's actual involvement in or expressed desire to be involved in acts of violence, male comrades still perceived women to be frail and afraid:

> *Females are expected to clean and all that. They are not energetic, if I can put it that way. They are not strong and all that because of the way they are treated and all. So I don't think for them to be part of this violence is correct. They are not strong. (Sello)*

Sello implies that young women comrades are 'weak' and unable to deal with 'hard violence'. As a result, in his view, they represent themselves as less intrepid than their male counterparts.

# Organising political violence

The 'organising' of political violence by comrade youth is rooted in the '80s period of ungovernability. Acts of violence, and the liberatory political organisations using it, were illegal. The policy of the legal UDF◊ was formally one of non-violence. As a result, the technicalities for carrying out acts of political violence were never discussed in its affiliated organisations. Political violence would be discussed in meetings in an almost academic or abstract manner:

> *During the times of ungovernability, we sat down and looked at our targets – councillors, policemen, even cars that used to deliver goods from town. So obviously we tried to explain to our constituencies what their targets were. So in those ways we tried to collaborate with the call by the liberation movement for ungovernability. (Thabo)*

The technical planning of these actions happened outside of formal meetings. Key formal leaders could not be seen to be involved in the organisation of

---

◊ Sayco's 1987 draft policy document, for example, states: 'Sayco is committed to non-violent and non-racial methods of struggle against colonialism … As a legal mass organisation, our commitment to non-violent methods of struggle is imperative and principled.'

political violence. This would implicate the organisation itself in violence and would place the entire youth leadership in danger:

> *Those people who co-ordinated political violence, some were leaders of organisations and some were not. Let's say the executive committee – they will not co-ordinated such underground things because the minute that information leaks that the people are members of the executive committee, that organisation will immediately be in danger because their leadership is involved in some of these things. (Thabo)*

Political violence, particularly in the '80s, was guided by political objectives. There was a clear enemy for the youth during this period. Targets constituting the enemy were identified within formal meetings. Actual tactics for carrying our specific acts of violence were decided on outside the meetings:

> *When we talk of targets, we had lectures to identify our aims. But we never in a single meeting said we are going to attack a particular house or such a policeman, because that contradicts our constitution which says we are a non-violent organisation. Such things only happened after our meetings … Only a few people would know what was going to happen. After the meeting we would just go to the policeman, the people in front throwing stones, attack and then move to another place. In our meetings we were not doing those things as members of Cosas or Soyco, but as the youth of South Africa supporting the call of the ANC. (Lumkile)*

As part of the tactical planning of violence, a few youth were identified to lead a particular act. Other youth would take the cue from these 'leaders'.

According to the youth I interviewed, there were two groups of leadership during the period of 'people's war'. First, there were those who were above ground and formal – 'strategic leadership'. Second there were those who headed the practical organisation of political violence – 'technical leadership':

> *Individuals planned these things for the sake of not putting our organisation in danger. Those people made underground plans. Each and every country when it is involved in a revolutionary situation talks of strategic leadership and technical leadership. So technical leadership are the ones who sort of work underground. So we moved in groups making sure that every group had disciplined comrades who led that group to that particular point, did what they had to do and dispersed. (Thabo)*

The '80s activists in Diepkloof had a very strong sense of commitment to their organisations and would not jeopardise them by implicating them openly in acts of political violence.

The activist youth had a clear sense of which individuals were planning and co-ordinating the acts of violence that were to be implemented. Different individuals were known as heading certain geographical areas or zones in Diepkloof. The youth would simply watch for the signals from that person. After meetings, youth comrades would take their cues and action would follow, after which the group would quickly break up. During the process of carrying out these actions, the youth who had not been in meetings would form a part of the group and participate in whatever was happening at the time. After action had taken place, the various co-ordinators would meet and report on what had occurred and whether there had been any problems:

> *What would happen is that we would separate ourselves. You see in Diepkloof we have zones. Then maybe X is in charge of Zone 1 and M is in charge of Zone 4 and so on. So in that way we were able to make things easier, because at the end of the day we will come together and discuss the problems we encountered with the different zones. By then the majority of youth were prepared to participate in these structures. So what we needed was only direction, you know. Decisions to burn an office or something would not be discussed in a meeting, you know. People who knew the targets would be in the front after the meeting. They would lead and the rest would follow. They will see the leaders maybe at the police station. And we at the front will start to throw stones or maybe another missile, then they will also start to throw missiles. But it's not a plan from the meeting, it just happened. (Lumkile)*

As with other campaigns, there was also a concern with trying to avoid spontaneous and unco-ordinated action:

> *I don't want to believe that in the '80s things were just spontaneous. I believe there was always a directive. There was no way someone could just go out and not account for what happened. No, there was a prescription. Leadership would say what was relevant. That was the bottom line. (Namedi)*

The organising of collective political violence was incredibly complex and sophisticated. What is perhaps most astonishing about the intricate plans that were formulated was the fact that most of the youth involved were extremely young, many still at school.

## Constraining the comrades

Older members of the community did not, interestingly enough, perceive excessive and seemingly meaningless violence to have stemmed from the activities of organised youth. They believed the more contentious acts of violence to be the work of youths not subject to the discipline of these organisations – in other words, criminal elements.

One Diepmeadow councillor told me:

> Youth in political organisations you can reason with. They give you time to discuss. They are prepared to talk to you … The youth who are emotional are the ones involved in violence. The ANC Youth League are not so much violent. The problem is when they start to mix with the criminal youth.

Probably more than any other action in the '80s, political violence was something over which youth leadership had the most difficulty exerting control. This problem arose in the absence of technical leadership:

> *In some cases other people took advantage, doing their own thing, and later they said the comrades did it, even though there were no comrades there – only individuals misusing the name of struggle while doing their own personal thing. (Thabo)*

As mentioned earlier, it was not only the unemployed but also school-going youth – organisationally not disciplined, yet caught up in the mood of ungovernability – who caused problems for students more generally:

> *During school days, you see other guys will go and burn cars outside and we are in classes. When the police come, we are being teargassed for nothing. When we ask what is wrong. You know, unplanned action, you see. But now it affects the whole organisation and we feel there are very reactionary students. Then people say, comrades don't want to go to school, because now comrades are not learning. (Lumkile)*

Youth activists would then try to track down the culprits and deal with them in ways they thought most appropriate:

> *Now we talk to these youth and say that we do not understand that these things must be done, but we have to do this in a correct manner, disciplined manner and you don't have to do this as individuals. We have to do this but as the whole student body. But, you see, maybe some youth will repeat the very same thing tomorrow. Then maybe we will have to take stronger measures, disciplining them. (Lumkile)*

'Inappropriate' actions were often responded to with mechanical discipline, agreed upon by a disciplinary committee of the youth organisations. The main concern of youth activists was to bring all youth under the control of the organisations:

> *Even in the '80s violence was spontaneous to some extent. Certain people were giv-*
> *ing orders. People would not necessarily account for their actions. The leadership*
> *would give certain orders after a meeting. You would decide which way to go. The*
> *leaders would give orders what was to be done and after that it was spontaneous.*
> *There would be some people who took part in violence but they were not disciplined*
> *members of organisation. However, something would happen to these people if you*
> *did not act properly in those days. (Musi)*

These kinds of activities were assessed by youth activists. If they were deemed
to be within the broad aims of the liberation movement, an attempt would be
made to incorporate the youth into existing youth structures. Youth involved
in activities considered 'counter-revolutionary' would face other consequences.
There was a very clear sense of an ever-present leadership both giving direction and bringing the youth to order when activities were deemed problematic:

> *We would look at the kind of action that is being taken and whether that action is*
> *progressive or counter-progressive. We will maybe meet with them, encourage them*
> *to carry on with the job, but to join the masses. They mustn't go on their own. They*
> *must be seen within the masses, you know. And those who are doing the wrong*
> *thing, I don't want to lie to you, they were disciplined very highly by sjambokking.*
> *(Lumkile)*

In Diepkloof, there is evidence to suggest intolerance of any attempts by other
organisations to organise youth in the township. This was a result of the
Charterist's hegemonic project to bring all township youth into the Charterist
fold. Youth in Alexandra township had similar plans and were deeply suspicious of other political groupings, such as the Azanian People's Organisation
(Azapo). Ongoing and violent battles ensued between UDF-affiliated and
Azapo-affiliated youth in Alexandra (Carter, 1991).

It is not clear whether the intolerance of other political groupings in
Diepkloof led to violent encounters. What was clear, however, was that the
comrade youth made organising by other groupings very difficult:

> *We never allowed Azapo to operate here. In fact I still remember that Azapo [Azanian*
> *Students' Movement] wanted to come here to organise and we told them clearly that*
> *you see here in Diepkloof we are organising under the banner of Sosco. By then*
> *Cosas was banned. We told them here we are organised under the banner of Sosco*
> *and if you come here to organise, your area is going to divide us, you see. So maybe,*
> *please, leave our area in peace. And those comrades were not from this area, they*
> *were from Orlando, you see and then they left. (Lumkile)*

What this kind of exclusionary behaviour did do, however, was to make the presence of the UDF-affiliated organisations such as Cosas, Soyco and the civic very obvious. Youth and townships residents were closely observed and codes of conduct enforced. This in turn limited the potential for spontaneous occurrences of political violence in the '80s.

The decreased organisational capacity of youth organisations in the early '90s meant that the nature of collective violence changed significantly. Political violence became increasingly undirected, unaccountable and spontaneous. The breakdown in organisational structures of accountability also led to small groups of youth – sometimes even individual youth – being involved in acts of violence with no collective consent or back-up. In three separate incidents in Diepkloof in 1991, individual youth – who belonged to the ANCYL or Cosas – attempted on their own to ambush police vehicles. In each case, they lost their lives.

The lack of accountability and vigilance went further than youth engaging in acts of direct violence. On 12 March 1992 I wrote in my diary about an event that disturbed me greatly:

> Earlier this afternoon Zola told me he wanted to show me something. He told me a 'target' was supposed to come the night before but didn't and he wanted to show me something to help me understand … I followed him to his room. He went inside the house and came out with a bag. He closed the door and took out a huge rifle. I just looked at this thing and said nothing. I asked him whether he was part of a defence unit. He said he was not – he operated on his own … I asked him why he had told me about the gun. He replied that this was because I was his best friend and he trusted me … I then asked him where he had got the rifle from … He had got the gun from a white home which he had robbed the previous month. He said that he watched the house for a few days and he knew when the people were out. He then entered the house and took the gun. He took nothing else as he was scared since this was his first time to do such a thing. He had gone alone … I asked him where he had got the idea to do such a thing from. He told me that Vuyani had once given him a tape with speeches by Tambo from the '80s. Vuyani died before he could copy the tape. He now keeps the tape as a special article left to him by Vuyani. According to him the tape now gives him guidance in the absence of Vuyani. I asked him if he ever discussed the guidance of this tape with

anyone in his organisation. He says he has not and that no one except me knows he has the weapon. Zola does not see it as problematic that the tape was made of speeches of people's war in the '80s. He sees it as still relevant today. He sees himself as needing to defend the community 'who I love all of them and I must protect them any time'.

A number of deductions can be drawn from this account. For Zola, political violence – in much the same form it existed in the '80s – was still appropriate. However, there was no leadership person with whom he could openly share his ideas and plan tactical activities. Whatever his activities were, these were likely to be unsupported (practically) by other members of his organisation. His actions would only be known about after the deed, and would not be subjected to organisational goals and discipline. The fact that he showed me the rifle indicates a lack of discretion and discipline. This action appears to separate his behaviour from that of the comrade youth in the '80s. As the ANCYL's secretary general, Rapu Molekane, put it:

> In the '80s if you had a gun, you didn't tell anyone. Now it's the fashion. Whereas the thugs of the past could be disciplined by organisations, those of today are armed, dangerous and untouchable. (*The Weekly Mail*, 29 May 1992)

It should be noted that Zola was thought of as a leader by newly organised youth in his zone in Diepkloof. Shortly after this incident, police tried to arrest him. Zola subsequently skipped the country to join Umkhonto we Sizwe in one of the frontline states.

According to youths who were activists in the '80s, violence in the early '90s had become increasingly spontaneous. The change in the ANC's strategies and tactics led to confusion and a lack of clear direction from leadership at all levels. There was consequently confusion about why certain acts of violence happened at all:

> *Today, youth are not able to understand what is happening. Youth react out of anger. They have not been discussing and some act out of frustration and not out of understanding what the leadership are saying ... The reality is that youth disarm without direction ... In the '90s there is no explanation as to why action happens. There are very few people engaged in these things. People can no longer account in terms of their objectives. (Namedi)*

Many of the acts of violence carried out by the youth in Diepkloof in the early '90s seemed poorly planned with a lack of clarity about how the stated intent of these actions correlated with the incident of violence itself. I have already mentioned the attack on the oil tanker. After hearing several contradictory explanations, I was not convinced of the link between the tanker and the struggle to decrease the cost of school fees.

One of the few youth leaders of the '80s who was still participating in youth structures in Diepkloof in the early '90s, made this statement:

> *No one can condone such actions. There must be an explanation. Those actions that are taking place are not well co-ordinated. People in leadership are not there when these things are happening. If youth feel there is no response to their demands, they take action which is not well defined. (Namedi)*

The spiralling comtsotsi phenomenon in the early '90s also made it increasingly difficult for youth organisations to ascertain who had carried out various acts of political violence. It was very difficult to bring these youth to order.

By June 1993, this had become a national problem – particularly in relation to local Self Defence Units (SDUs) in which youth were centrally involved. These problems led the ANC to resolve at a summit to take extensive disciplinary measures against criminal elements who were playing destructive and dangerous roles in such structures.

According to the *Sowetan* of 23 November 1992, the ANC identified problems with SDUs in the Vaal as

> ... intense infiltration by agent provocateurs, a lack of accountability to democratic structures and a lack of experience and organisation. The summit agreed that lack of discipline and training gave rise to car hijackings, rape, extortion, bribery and murder.

The decreased capacity of youth organisations and leaders to direct and control collective violence was a source of concern for political leaders, activists and, in fact, all communities in South Africa in the early '90s. At no point, however, did these problems lead to a situation of anarchy or real chaos in Diepkloof – the apocalypse that some predicted never happened. Perhaps this was because youth organisations did retain some of their 'moral integrity' and ability to assert authority over the youth who called themselves comrades. But, perhaps it was also because the young men and women who engaged in acts of political violence continued to have clear justifications for their actions. The next chapter explores the various justifications that were given by these youth.

112

# CHAPTER 8

# 'We are fighting for the liberation of our people': Justifications of violence

To understand why the youth participated in acts of political violence, it is necessary to develop insight into how they symbolised violence in their own minds and interpreted this into language. As Stanage (1974: 222) has pointed out, 'language is the most distinctive human activity whereby persons become conscious of their feelings'. This chapter looks at how activist and comrade youth in Diepkloof represented political violence, especially with regard to its perceived morality. This representation is integrally linked to what it meant to be a 'youth' and a 'comrade'.

Experiences of, and engagement in, acts of violence tended to generate their own discourse. The youth developed a discourse relating to the violence in their day-to-day experience. It was a combination of the official liberation movement literature (both legal and illegal), leaders' statements, literature about liberation struggles in other countries such as Mozambique and Cuba, as well as their own political memories as participants in the struggle. The discourse was political and moral in content. It both coincided with and contradicted the ideology and identity of the broader Charterist social movement.

The youth I interviewed, in justifying and understanding political violence, made constant use of a number of key words and phrases. The word 'target' referred to people and objects 'deserving' of physical attack. Other prevalent terms were 'people's war' and 'ungovernability'. Everyone I interviewed spoke about 'the community', which usually meant Diepkloof residents but was sometimes as broad in its parameters as African people in South Africa. The youth referred to themselves as 'comrades', signifying 'moral defenders of the community'. Closely linked to the idea of being a comrade was that of being a 'youth'. To be a 'youth' meant to be 'energetic' and 'vigorous' and hence able to engage in a variety of activities. Finally, the notion of 'correct' was used frequently. It referred to behaviour and beliefs seen to be of high 'moral' standing, and was inextricably linked to the comrade identity. There were six main justifications given by the youth for their involvement in political violence:

- First, they perceived themselves as having responded earlier to the ANC's call to take up armed struggle as a strategy for change – this was still seen as relevant in the early '90s.

- Second, they believed the root of violence lay in the direct and structural violence of the state, particularly the activities of the police.
- Third, they believed 'real liberation' was not possible without bloodshed – hence the mistrust of the negotiations process and the continuation of speeches carried over from the '80s into the '90s.
- Fourth, they felt it logical that the youth, as defenders of the community and their prime position in the liberation struggle, would and should be involved in acts of political violence.
- Fifth, they believed violence would speed up the process of change.
- Sixth, they felt they held the moral high ground and could thus maintain unity, or political hegemony, through the use of violence against those who were seen as being outside of the morality of organised youth or the liberation movement more broadly.

While each of these justifications will be examined separately, they are integrally linked to one another. They formed part of a coherent discourse that could be threaded together from the language of the Diepkloof youth.

# Responding to the call of the ANC

In the '80s, Diepkloof's youth organisations had a prime goal: to end apartheid. The Charterist social movement more broadly understood that this was not going to happen simply by politicising activists and the community.

Organisations had to develop mass bases and take action to challenge the very legitimacy and functional capacity of the state. This meant going beyond the regular boycotts and calls for resignation of corrupt councillors into more serious acts of civil disobedience. Cosas and Sayco both strongly identified with the ANC and its 'four pillars of struggle'. These were: building up and consolidating internal structures; mobilising the masses around issues to increase political awareness and build support; international isolation; and stepping up military activities around Umkhonto we Sizwe (Phillips, 1988).

Acts of violence against both state property and people became a logical extension of these four pillars, reinforced by the ANC's 1985 call to 'make the country ungovernable'. Youth responded to this call willingly. They were confronted with violence on a day-to-day basis and their chances for educational advancement and employment were poor. They were also provoked by the constant and violent presence of the security forces in the township and in the school grounds. 'Smashing the apartheid state' was welcomed as a potential path to freedom.

While Sayco and Cosas claimed to be non-violent, in their public statements they promoted the youth as 'young lions' who, according to Sayco's draft policy document in 1987: '... form the core of the 'political' and 'military' armies of the revolution. Their youthful energy enables them to perform great feats in the theatre of battles ...' The youth in Diepkloof took up the role of the 'young lions'. As Thabo stated: 'We carried out violence against the state, not as Cosas members, but as the youth of South Africa supporting the call of the ANC.'

However, the cultural repertoire of armed struggle outlived strategic reality. The ANC suspended armed struggle in 1990 when it entered into negotiations with the state. But within the ANC itself during this period, the suspension of armed struggle was precarious. Several MK commanders, such as Abobaker Ishmail and Riaz Saloojee, later successfully sought amnesty from the TRC for continuing to supply weapons within the country between 1991 and 1994, arguing in their applications that communities still needed to be defended against the violence of the 'state and its surrogates' (*Daily Mail*, 15 August 2000).

At the local level, in places like Diepkloof, there was confusion and controversy as to whether the armed struggle should have been suspended at the time. In the early '90s, while there were many youth who believed armed struggle was still a necessary pillar of struggle, there were others who believed revolutionary violence against the regime was no longer appropriate. These differing views were reflected in a dialogue I listened to and recorded between two Diepkloof youth in June 1992:

> *Sello: The youth have the same role today as in the '80s. At that time the ANC told us we should make the country ungovernable. So today I think that thing it is still the same precisely because the government tyrants are ungovernable themselves. It is the same problems as before.*
>
> *Namedi: You see, this is a problem when we still have our own comrades saying there is not change. But there are changes and because of these changes we need to adapt a new style of working and develop new targets and strategies ... In the past we had to render the state ungovernable ... Now we need to start to think objectively because of the changed conditions.*

The ideological divisions referred to in Chapter 6 gave rise to similar divisions in attitude towards political violence, particularly revolutionary violence. Youth such as Namedi (a member of the 1985 Detachment), as disciplined ANC supporters, were generally more prepared to redefine the strategies and tactics of the youth in the 'new era'. These youth, while wary of the negotiations process, were 'trying to think objectively because of the changed conditions'. They were in the minority.

The majority of youth I interviewed were angry and frustrated with the negotiation process. Like Sello, they believed the state remained a 'tyrant' that was ungovernable – unable to govern the country. The ANC's strategy of 'ungovernability' remained, for them, as applicable in the early '90s as it was in the '80s.

## The oppressive state

More than anything else, it was the violent nature of the security forces and the youths' direct daily experiences of this violence that led to their serious questioning of non-violence as a viable strategy:◊

> *I can say the police contributed more to our youth being violent. It's just like the handling of unrest situations ... I remember there was a time in '86 there was a stayaway organised by Bishop Tutu. So there we organised a march here in Diepkloof. So without provocation our youth were shot, people were arrested and people were brutally assaulted. So now the culture of violence started there. (Lumkile)*

Peaceful marches, says Lumkile, became violent when police began to shoot at the youth. Police violence was compounded by the arrests, brutal treatment, assaults and even killings of the youth and other 'people'. Lumkile believed these actions by the state security forces precipitated the 'culture of violence' in the youth.

Many youth I interviewed felt that, besides police violence, the police also took from people what was rightfully theirs. The police carried out the policies of the state, ensuring the continued deprivation of black South Africans. There was structural violence as well as direct violence. The notion of 'rights' was pervasive in these youths' consciousness. As Chris said:

> *Violence comes from maybe the police themselves depriving people of maybe their rights. At times they even harass people like going to a funeral and all that.*

---

◊   This is in line with both the understandings of Seekings (1988, 1992) and Tilly et al (1975). These works propose that repression often leads to resistance and more confrontational forms of conflict. It should also be noted that the ANC itself believed in non-violent collective action as a strategy for change for many decades. This changed with the 1960 Sharpeville massacre. Police opened fire on a peaceful protest against passes, killing 69 people. The government subsequently banned the ANC and other liberation organisations.

Thus, through their actions of physical violence, police denied township residents their 'rights', their liberty to engage in everyday activities. The harassment of people going to a funeral – a sacred event – was given as an example of this denial of human rights, and was deserving of retaliation.

Not just the police but the broader state itself, not surprisingly, was viewed negatively. The state was defined as the 'apartheid' or 'racist' regime – not particularly as a capitalist entity. It was seen as having created inequalities between the various racial groupings in South Africa. Musi told me: 'This racist government of apartheid has caused separation; racially, tribal and all that and lack of equalness between these groups.'

The state was viewed as coercive, as having ensured that black people were deprived of their basic rights. As Nika said: 'The worst thing about this government is that our people have no right, having no vote, in fact have no say in anything whatever.'

Finally, the state was responsible for limiting individuals in the 'African community' from developing socially and economically. Thabo stated that:

> *This apartheid government has disrupted most of my plans, especially for my future because maybe today I must be something; like I could finish university or college. But due to apartheid, most of my plans haven't hatched.*

The inequalities of apartheid society, together with the coercion used by the security forces to uphold an illegitimate regime, were at the root of most youths' understanding of the etiology of political violence:

> *This government is not our government. So the killing will never stop. Why? Because this government is a thug ... So if the place is ruled by thugs, the killing will never stop. In Russia there is no crime. Why? Because the government was appointed by the people. (Zola)*

Embedded in this quote is the assumption that state representivity is a prerequisite for peace. If the government were democratically elected, violence would no longer be necessary. The South African state was a 'thug' – a bully that took from people what was rightfully theirs. In Zola's view, the state in Russia, by comparison, was 'good' since it represented a 'people's government'.

A further justification for violence was that the Diepkloof youth perceived themselves as relatively deprived in comparison with others, particularly those with wealth:

> *South Africa is a violent society because you see there are people who are enjoying privileges and there are people who are not enjoying privileges, you see. So in fact at*

> *this present time of course South Africa is a violent society due to what I have stated ... Others have not got their rights and culture. They have been destroyed ... So there can be no peace ... (Musi)*

Musi indicated an understanding of class inequality in the society. Unequal privileges meant the society was structurally violent at its base. The rights and even the culture of poor people – everything that was meaningful to them in their everyday existence – had been destroyed.

While peaceful means were seen as admirable, the use of violence by the security forces led these youth to believe that non-violence was an inappropriate and unfeasible strategy for change. Lumkile told me: 'Comrades say now we are peaceful, and those people [the police] are fighting. So what's the use of being peaceful?' He assumes that when confronting an intensely violent state and its security forces, violence is the only retaliatory strategy that has the potential to lead to serious attention to the grievances and demands of the oppressed.

Violence as a retaliatory strategy – retributive justice – was considered by many to be the only way to get the state to pay attention to the grievances and demands of the oppressed:

> *Then people retaliate because they just can't take the police harassing them. So people themselves got fed up, then they decided to retaliate ... How they retaliate I can't exactly say, but they will do any form of retaliation they can think of. They might throw the police with stones and all that. (Chris)*

'Striking back' on behalf of the community was seen to be a defensive act, rather than an offensive one. It was justifiable in the face of the morally indefensible actions of others, such as the security forces. Peace was not possible until inequality had been eradicated through 'fighting'. As Musi stated: 'Violence will always be the order of the day because, you see, we Africans always fight to make sure we retain our rights and our culture.'

Acts of violence were important as a means of regaining dignity, said other youth. Youth believed that collective violence was both a rational and inevitable response to state violence, and consequently they absolved themselves from the responsibility resulting from their engagement in violence. They were merely responding to an 'evil' that confronted them as township residents.

While political violence was seen as a rational response, the discourse used indicated that the responsibility for political violence perpetrated by the youth lay solely with the state. The unintended consequence of this is that these young people denied themselves as real actors. This denial is threaded throughout their discourse and accounts of political violence.

# Bloodshed is necessary for liberation

Frantz Fanon wrote extensively during his life about the 'psychology of the oppressed' and suggested that involvement in military and often violent activities for national liberation could have a healing or transforming effect on individuals. Straker (1992), in trying to find a psychological explanation for the involvement of youth in political violence, found no evidence that participation in violence was viewed as 'healing'.

But a number of Diepkloof youth I interviewed clearly believed there could be no real liberation without violence and bloodshed:

> *Violence is needed in our country so we can remove all the bad things that are there. This present regime is like a sickness that must be destroyed violently so that better things can exist and the society can be more healthy. So violence is necessary. (Musi)*

Violence had a cleansing effect since it represented the elimination of what was evil and unsanitary. Apartheid was a 'sickness' that, if not 'destroyed', would contaminate a new society. The need for violence, youth asserted, was common to all liberation struggles. They were well aware of the histories of liberation in places such as Cuba, Nicaragua, Mozambique, Namibia and Angola, and glorified the 'violent' revolutions that had taken place in these countries. In a sense, they had an almost Sorelian approach to violence: ◊

> *There is no easy road to freedom.* * What we are experiencing right now is what Namibia also experienced before it was liberated and all that. And then I will never be surprised if there is a civil war maybe next year in South Africa. (Chris)*

The perception that violence or war was a necessary part of transition gave rise to the exaltation of casualties on both sides. The death of someone associated with apartheid was seen as a move one step closer to liberation. Zola told me: 'To kill a policeman is to mean we are closer to our freedom because we are getting rid of some of the obstacles of our struggle.' The loss of life of a comrade, however, was an example of an exemplary soldier or 'freedom fighter' prepared to give up his or her life for the betterment of the country. As Thandi said:

> *Many comrades, like Vuyani, have died in our struggle for liberation. But these comrades are true heroes and freedom fighters who have died because they loved their country so much.*

---

◊   For Sorel 'it was not a question of justifying violence but of understanding its role in history. Great historic action was inevitably marked by violence' (Roth, 1980: 50).

*   This sentence is a direct quote from Nelson Mandela at the famous Rivonia trial of 1964.

Death and sacrifice were thus part of both the discourse and practice of political violence.

# Violence as necessary for 'real change'

There was a strong belief that, without violence, change would be incremental and incomplete. Most youths were sceptical of the negotiations process – they doubted the sincerity of the apartheid government. As a result, they were not convinced by the ANC's decision to suspend the armed struggle, especially when people in the townships continued to die in the early '90s. Thabo stated: 'It was a blunder for the ANC to suspend the armed struggle because of violence, the killing of our people.'

Even those youth in Cosas and the ANCYL who did support negotiations felt frustrated by the ANC's slow route to remove apartheid. As Sipho said:

> … comrades have been patient trying to solve things through negotiations … the comrades they try to compromise. But practically we see there is a problem, practically.

In the early '90s the state was still in control of the security forces and continued to carry out acts of violence against township residents. The 'masses' had no real defence against this large, repressive force. Sipho remarked to me: 'The state is still having its machinery which it uses against the people. This state machinery is large and we still find the masses fighting with stones.'

The changes that had taken place were viewed as spurious. While the comrades had compromised, the state was intact. 'Real change' entailed overthrowing the government. In the early '90s, patience was running out; there was a sense of urgency. As Sello said:

> The thing that will ultimately bring change is the overthrowment of the regime. This is feasible since it is directly proportional to our efforts … The structures do not yet exist for this, but we are working toward this.

Sello implied that other forms of struggle – such as negotiations and international pressure – were less important than armed struggle for bringing about change. The apartheid state was not a negotiating partner – it was an institution that needed to be vanquished. Although Sello admitted that organisational structures were very weak in the early '90s, he believed that with more 'exertion' and greater organisation on the part of the youth organisations, insurrection in South Africa was possible.

The need to remove the state violently for immediate change – before the liberation movement completely compromised itself, to its own detriment – was directly linked to the perception that political violence was necessary to 'cleanse' the society of all that was bad and evil. There was definitely a desire for a more fundamental kind of change than it seemed the outcome of negotiations would produce.

## The youth as defenders of the community

Self-identity – as comrades, as youth and as the 'bearers' of the future – motivated young activists to engage in struggle. They felt they were in the rightful position to lead the struggle towards a new and better society. Xolile told me:

> *We as the youth know that the future is in our hands because the old men, Nelson Mandela, Oliver Tambo, will disappear because they are old. Therefore the people who are going to be responsible for the future South Africa will be the youth.*

The youth knew that the future would lie in the hands of the younger generation. The 'old men' were going to die and the future would then be their responsibility. They had many hopes for a new and better society. They wanted peace, democracy, economic wealth, proper education and a non-racial society. Thabo told me: 'We want to have a future based on the Freedom Charter where the most important thing is to have non-racialism.'

Because the youth saw themselves as 'energetic', 'flexible', 'agile' and 'adaptable',◊ they were positioned to defend the community against perceived outside dangers and threats. These were wider than just the activities of the state. Gangs and Inkatha, as we have already seen, led to an almost functional necessity for youths to be engaged in a variety of forms of political violence:

> *You know a youth, if you tell a youth about violence like you say, 'hey there's Inkatha coming in this direction', hey they never going to stop to go there. Hey, they are leaving the school ... they saying they want to fight ... they say they are going to defend our masses. (Bheki)*

---

◊ These youth 'attributes' were identified in Sayco's draft policy document in the '80s: 1. 'the young and rising generation constitutes a representative of the future in the broadest sense'; 2. 'the stage of youth is one of learning and assimilating'; 3. 'the youth is enthusiastic ... determined, impatient and displays great zeal and verve in fighting for what it conceives as just'; 4. 'young people can be easily swayed into positions'.

It seems that moving towards sites of perceived danger was an automatic reaction for the youth. They played a significant role in shielding the community and their 'masses' from outside threat of any kind. Diepkloof was their geographic territory that they needed to protect. The 'community' was 'good' – not part of Inkatha or the gangster formations.

Their role as warriors was seen as far more important than their role as school-goers. They found it difficult to remain in a classroom while warlike activities were taking place on the streets outside. Straker accurately describes the dissonance in the day-to-day lives of the township youth which led to their conflictive responses. She says, of the youth she interviewed:

> They were not conscripted soldiers within a conventional army fighting battles in a combat zone. Yet they were engaged in what they saw as a civil war ... At the same time, the youth were meant to attend school as usual and to carry on their daily affairs. (Straker, 1992: 111)

Despite the high rate of unemployment in Diepkloof, the youth still perceived 'adults' as parents who had jobs – and who were outside of the township for a large part of the time:

> *The people who are experiencing the violence are the youth because the youth are the ones who are in the location full time. They can see everything that is happening, but their parents are not there, they work. The youth must defend their properties. (Xolile)*

The youth had to hold the fort while their parents were away. They were the 'eyes' and 'ears' of the community. Without their vigilance and activities, the township would be without protection against gangsters or potential enemies such as Inkatha:

> *Youth is the one who is involved in political violence. While I have just stated that youth is militant then I mean if you remain as a resident of Diepkloof, then you can't just be doing nothing. I can't accept that maybe Inkatha do attack us. Instead of attacking us, then we will also avenge ourselves. Then the parents they used to be sleeping, then the youth go and fight. (Chris)*

The parents worked during the day, the youth worked at night. Adults were passive, youth were militant. In the face of attack, from Inkatha or any external threat, the youth could not remain inactive. Political violence on behalf of the community was considered to be retaliatory and provoked.

# Holding the moral high ground

Youth who engaged in the liberation struggle didn't only believe they were defending the community in a physical sense. They felt they were also defending the 'morality' of the township, and in doing so, building unity or homogeneity. They wanted to preserve what was good in the township. Being 'moral' meant not committing crimes against other community members. Crimes such as theft, rape and murder caused suspicion and fear and led to 'disunity'. This was problematic in the struggle since, to achieve a common 'good', people had to work toward a common goal. 'Cleansing' the community was necessary for the youths' 'liberatory project' (Scharf & Ngcokoto, 1990: 341).

In earlier chapters I have shown how those who identified with the liberation movement were expected to act in a 'disciplined' way. Behaving in an 'undisciplined' manner involved harming either an organisation or the community in some way. It also had a negative impact on unity. For mass struggle to be effective, communities needed to be consolidated against a common enemy, not divided within. As the oppositional force, the liberation movement and its followers had to be seen to be morally superior so as to be worth supporting. When people did the 'wrong thing', they had to be punished or 'disciplined' – as we have already explored. 'Irredeemable' offenders could expect death as a punishment:

> The comrades solve a problem. Other boys they don't understand, they need help. But other boys they didn't understand when the comrades talk, so that's why the comrades have killed them. If a comrade tell a person what is bad and they don't understand, she must kill them because she is going to do bad things like killing my grandmother and stealing money from my sisters. (Thandi)

The horrifying consequence that Thandi claimed was necessary for those who did not understand what was right and what was wrong was – potentially – death. This emerged from a belief that such a lack of understanding meant there was a likelihood that crimes would be committed in the future. The comrade youth felt it was their duty to put these offenders on the right path, or to remove them if they presented a serious enough threat to the community, especially to those most vulnerable – women and the elderly.

Violence was seen as a pre-emptive and also preventive method. Killing someone meant that person would not be able to harm others again. It was also a warning to others as to what to expect from the comrades for 'wrongdoings'.

Despite the justifications for violence implicit in the youth's discourse, they did not desire violence or relish being involved in it. They saw it as a 'necessary evil' towards a political end – bringing an end to apartheid rule:

> *I don't think the youth want to be involved in violence. Really, it is bad and no one mentally fit can support violence. So I don't think youth in this country maybe enjoys or wants to be involved in violence, but they are prepared maybe to make sure that this violence comes to an end because it makes most of the things they enjoy to be impossible. So this is why I'm saying that no human being who is mentally all right can support violence. Only those who are perpetrating it can want to see it prevailing every day. (Nika)*

Political violence was instrumental – it was a means for achieving political gains. Nika believed that violence by the state and other agents could only be ended through counter-violence. Violence carried out either by the state, or by gangsters, or by undisciplined elements, prevented the youth from 'enjoying' life. But, Nika asserted, no one likes violence either. To do so would be absurd, even an indication of mental illness. In fact, violence was seen as something 'tough' which had to be done:

> *No one likes to fight. To fight is not to play. To fight is to fight and maybe if you are watching, you see it is hard. So you know that you can die. So then it is a lie if the press say that the youth are getting happy if they can be involved in those violence. You can only be happy if you have peace. We want peace and peace you must fight for it. (Zola)*

For Zola, violence was not a form of entertainment or something that was fun. Being involved in acts of violence was both physically and emotionally demanding, and there was a chance of the loss of life of people close to you. While violence may have been accepted as an indispensable facet of the struggle for 'peace', engaging in violence was accompanied by both mental and physical anguish.

Implicit in the language of the youth, however, were a number of worrying themes. First, as was mentioned earlier, there was evidence that the youth relinquished responsibility for their involvement in acts of collective violence – the causes and the problems that resulted from it lay outside of themselves. Second, they saw themselves as in some way 'morally advanced', and this self-perception had the potential to become the basic justification for their involvement in a wide range of activities. Third, if violence did outlive its strategic necessity, but continued to be employed, it could be used to achieve other goals or objectives – even those not endorsed by others in society, such as elders, political leaders and state authorities. It is for these reasons that youth involvement in criminal violence became a key concern for many South Africans in the early '90s, and continues to be a source of worry more than six years after the transition to democratic governance.

# CHAPTER 9

## Did Vuyani Mabaxa die in vain?

In April 1994 South Africans celebrated the inauguration of the first democratic, non-racial government in its history. Economic and political crises, international pressure, and the military activities of the liberation movement played crucial roles in this transition. However, what is too easily forgotten is that the metamorphosis that took place in South Africa was underpinned by a massive social movement opposed to apartheid rule. For the most part, organisations and members of this social movement were adherents of the Freedom Charter, a document drafted by the African National Congress together with other democratic organisations in 1955. It represented the hopes and aspirations of the majority of South Africans.

The backbone of this movement constituted residents of African townships throughout South Africa. The most active supporters and actors in this movement were African township youth, aged between 14 and 35. Thousands of youth in townships like Diepkloof were mobilised at the local level and were organised, by leaders such as Vuyani, to engage in campaigns and other collective activities against apartheid governance. This they did, often at their peril. They were detained for extended periods without being charged, forced to spend months in hiding, maimed by the brutal force of the security forces and many were killed.

Structural and direct violence were met with collective violence, carried out by the township youth. People or property symbolising the apartheid state, as well as individuals who threatened the cohesiveness of the township or the hegemony of the Charterist movement, were targeted and attacked, verbally abused, beaten and sometimes killed. While these collective actions were not always well organised and controlled (particularly in the early '90s), they were always purposive and rational.

Collective violence carried out by the youth who were supporters of the Charterist movement in Diepkloof became somewhat disorderly in the early '90s. Mobilised youth, who were less accountable and politically astute than those who were members of youth political organisations in the '80s, engaged in violent activities outside of the strict discipline and systems of accountability that had previously characterised youth organisations. This reflected the general decline that was taking place within the Charterist youth movement itself. The movement and its organisations had lost their most experienced

129

leadership, programmes of action were ill defined, and little direction was provided by regional and national bodies such as the ANCYL and the ANC itself.

The decline of a social movement like the Charterist youth movement is not surprising. All social movements have a career that is determined by both their internal dynamics and the external environment. Social movements are not static. They undergo a number of changes in their goals, structure, tactics, strategies and social base over time (Tilly, 1985). Social movements change dramatically when states change from authoritarian to democratic, as was the case in South Africa. Often their existence is closely linked to issues that relate specifically to the undemocratic nature of states (Mainwaring & Viola, 1984). With democratisation, social movements can become marginalised and isolated and their participants frustrated, disappointed and apathetic (Joppke, 1991).

The changed political climate of the '90s, to negotiations, shifted both the profile and the function of the Charterist social movement. It did not collapse, but it was no longer at the political centre stage and the strategies and tactics it had employed in the past were declared outmoded. The youth in Diepkloof who supported the Charterist movement seem to have found this transition a difficult one to make. Yet, they continued to believe they had a purpose, and that they had made an important contribution in the past.

While life in South Africa after the 1994 elections may not have brought with it real material changes in the lives of most black youth, the struggle for political liberation had been achieved. This is extremely important. ANCYL President Malusi Gigaba stated in February 2000: 'Happily, we enter the new century as a free people, having fulfilled the noble goal of our political emancipation'. This changed political arena is significant since, at least in principle, it opened the space for the participation of all youth in all areas of life and in all institutions of South African society. The focus of the youth movement changed and the issues placed on the agenda of the youth movement shifted from the political sphere to the social sphere.

In 1996, a National Youth Commission (NYC) was established. The Commission's brief was to help the government in developing a youth policy that would enhance job opportunities, skills training and education. Since 1998, the NYC has taken up a number of key projects. The most important of these have been an HIV/AIDS awareness programme, a skills and employment development programme, and the establishment of an interdepartmental committee to facilitate youth affairs in government.

The establishment of the NYC in itself is testimony to the role played by the youth in the liberation movement, the sacrifices they have made, and also an acknowledgement that the youth have very real needs that must be addressed.

However, the youth remained in abeyance after April 1994, 'caught within a new paradox; a freedom that offers few real opportunities' (Frank & Fisher, 1998: 7).

In 1997, the NYC conducted a study which found that 40 per cent of South African youth were neither employed nor in school. In Diepkloof too, most youth who formed part of this study were unemployed. They had left school before completing their studies, and were idle in the township with poor prospects for the future. According to Thabo Masebe of the ANCYL:

> The generation of 1976 was fighting for equality and against Bantu Education. Young people today have the opportunity in terms of education, but they are fighting for their jobs and other means of improving their lives. (*Weekly Mail & Guardian*, 13 June 1997)

The ANCYL in Diepkloof, and in fact nationally, never recovered from its decline in the early '90s. In 1998, the ANCYL's national conference in Johannesburg was characterised by much criticism and a diminishing membership. Critics accused the ANCYL of not doing much to influence policy formulation regarding youth. There was also an emphasis on the apathy of the youth (*Mail and Guardian*, 13 March 1998). This apathy was evident in the June 1999 second general election, when many young people (especially first-time voters) did not vote (Lodge, 1999). Some were disillusioned with politics, feeling that they had not reaped many benefits from the transition to democracy. Others were just not interested in the realm of politics, being more interested to live their lives as young people keen to have a good time and searching for exciting new experiences and life chances.

The membership of the ANCYL stood at 300 000 in July 2000. Alec Moemi, National Administrator of the ANCYL, argued in a telephonic interview with me in August 2000 that this number was not particularly low. He maintains that it is difficult to compare this number with the membership of Sayco in the '80s, since membership lists were not kept at that time. While this is true, there can be little doubt that Sayco was the largest affiliate of the UDF and was able to mobilise tens of thousands of youth in almost all local areas. In Diepkloof, the ANCYL had a membership of 120 in January 2000. This, according to Shimi Phati, provincial organiser of the ANCYL in Gauteng, was a huge downswing from the many thousands of youth who flocked to join the ANCYL in Diepkloof after the unbanning in February 1990. Cosas does still exist in Diepkloof, but only barely. It has a tiny membership and seems to organise in two of the schools only.

At the local level, the ANCYL struggled to develop campaigns and pro-grammes which could mobilise the youth from the mid '90s onwards. This in large part was the result of a lack of strong leadership who could take initia-tive at local level. Furthermore, according to Phati, many of the youth who could have led youth organisations were no longer available in the townships. They now worked and lived outside of the townships, and many schoolchil-dren were sent by their parents to schools in towns or in the suburbs.

The ANCYL and Cosas continue to exist and to organise, but they are vastly different from the organisations of the past. This is appropriate, given the changed environment in which they now operate. While in the past the youth mobilised around political issues, today they are more concerned with social issues. The main campaigns of the ANCYL in the year 2000 were AIDS awareness; anti-crime; environmental awareness, including access to water; the greening of cities; and anti-rape campaigns. Despite the centrality of these issues to the lives of young people in South Africa, these campaigns have failed to galvanise large numbers of youth in the same way that the political struggles of the past were able to do.

Sadly, AIDS has become the one issue that has the potential to mobilise the youth once more. In July 2000, AIDS researchers in South Africa pre-dicted that by the year 2010, about five million more people would die of AIDS. AIDS is having the most devastating toll on the economically ac-tive population between the ages of 15 and 49. Within this category, young women between the ages of 20 and 30 are most affected (*Sunday Times*, 9 July 2000).

The biggest enemy confronting the youth is no longer the repressive and oppressive state, but the AIDS epidemic. Journalist S'Thembiso Msomi says very different enemies were responsible for the death of young township resi-dents in the late '80s, as compared to the year 2000. He writes:

> It became our weekend ritual in the late '80's – attending two funerals on a Saturday and three more on a Sunday. At the cer-emonies we would learn of five more teenagers shot by the po-lice or a pupil stabbed to death by a vigilante group. It never seemed to stop ... The more schoolmates we buried, the closer the reality of death seemed to approach us. There seemed to be no place to hide. You could die for going to school, and you could die for staying at home. Now, six years after liberation, the killings have not stopped. Each weekend, an endless chain of overloaded passenger buses ferries mourners to the overflowing graveyard. Today we are crowded into this little primary school

classroom that acts as a community hall during weekends to bid farewell to the latest victim of the new vicious killer ... As we drive back from the graveyard, I wonder how many deaths it will take for this community to begin openly talking about AIDS. *(Sunday Times,* 18 June 2000)

AIDS had become public enemy number one of the youth by the year 2000. Appropriately then, HIV/AIDS became the focus of National Youth Day on 16 June 2000. The NYC, in particular, called on the youth to take a leading role in the struggle against AIDS. Prior to this, in December 1999, the youth in Soweto schools had launched a campaign called 'Youth on Top'. This campaign aimed to warn the youth about the dangers of AIDS, the importance of the use of condoms, and how to negotiate teenage sexuality (*Mail and Guardian,* 1 December 2000). The youth responded positively to the AIDS campaigns, and also to anti-crime campaigns and those aimed at job creation. But the numbers of youth who were mobilised were tiny compared to those that the Charterist youth movement was able to mobilise and organise prior to the 1994 elections.

# So, what has happened to the comrade youth of the past?

Did the decline in the Charterist youth movement and the continued lack of access of township youth to life chances mean that there was a slippery slide into the underworld of crime? Have yesterday's comrades become today's bandits? Some researchers and academics argue that this is the case. Amanda Dissel (1997), a researcher at the Centre for the Study of Violence and Reconciliation, argues that the non-delivery of material benefits by the government, together with these youth's prior training in the use of weapons and arms, led many youth in the direction of the underworld as a means of acquiring wealth. Similarly, Graeme Simpson believes unrealistic expectations of delivery have led to a rising crime rate that 'indicates growing disaffection, especially among the young' (1998: 2). Gangs, he argues, have become alternate providers of social cohesion.

There is a multiplicity of factors that have propelled some youth into a life of crime. These include broken homes, poverty, peer pressure, and feelings of relative deprivation. Furthermore, Segal, Pelo and Rampa argue that 'crime is one of the new forms of initiation into manhood for young boys in the urban setting of the township'(1999: 24). As crime becomes an organising focus of young people's lives, acts of crime become increasingly violent. This problem, of course, is worsened by the availability of guns in the townships, some of which were used in the '80s and early '90s by MK operatives and local youth 'defending' their communities. In Diepkloof, it was clear in the early '90s that weapons were in circulation among the activist youth.

■ **But are the youth who are involved in violent crime today the same youth who fought for political and social freedom?**
This is a difficult question to answer. It is clear that in Diepkloof there were cases where key activists from the '80s became known criminals in the early '90s. But, it is extremely difficult to ascertain exactly whether the majority of the youth who are currently engaged in criminal acts were politically active in the '80s and early '90s. This would be an interesting study in itself – speaking to young convicted criminals and finding out where they were during this period and what they were doing at the time. Were they in fact 'comrades'? Were they always involved in crime? Were they part of liberation military structures outside of South Africa? Were they kids who never really knew formal apartheid?

A second but related issue that needs to be examined is whether engagement in violence leads to a numbing which, in turn, makes future involvement in acts of violence unproblematic. Kerry Gibson, a South African child psychologist, asserted in the early '90s that 'violence does not beget violence in any sort of simple and direct fashion' (1991: 12). The fact that the comrade youth may have collectively killed a gangster, an informer, or an attacking Inkatha supporter, does not mean that they will easily hijack a random vehicle and murder the driver. Collective political violence carried out by the comrade youth in the past was driven by a set of clear moral justifications with stated political objectives. This is very different from the use of violence in self-interested and, by most accounts, indefensible acts of crime. Furthermore, as we saw in Chapter 8, Diepkloof youth experienced their involvement in violence as very disturbing. In their own words, violence is 'not a game', nor is it 'enjoyable'.

This is not to argue that no relationship exists between the comrade youth of the past and the criminal youth of the present. A link does seem to exist, but it not a straightforward one, and it seems to be limited to only some individuals. The Diepkloof case study shows that, as the ANCYL and Cosas became increasingly disorganised and undirected in the early '90s, the comtsotsi phenomenon became more apparent. For some of the youth, but by far the minority, the boundaries between political and criminal violence became blurred. Activists such as Lumkile, known as Slovo by the Diepkloof youth, became involved in gang activities and was killed in a gang war in late 1993. And Slovo was followed by some of his comrade supporters into a life of gangsterism. They took with them the military-like skills they had learned in the liberation movement, as well as the weapons they had acquired.

There are other examples of the slippery slide between activism and criminality. As mentioned previously, the early '90s was also a period when politicised youth, concerned with Third Force and vigilante activities in the townships, formed Self Defence Units (SDUs). SDUs were meant to have a special command and control system, and a paramilitary configuration, and members were to be trained by MK, the military wing of the ANC. The role of the SDUs was to defend communities against the hostel dwellers, mainly seen to be IFP-controlled, and the security forces. When SDUs were originally established, this was done with the full backing of the ANC and the SACP. But, by 1994, political parties were calling for the disbanding of these structures. Like the Charterist youth organisations at that time, many defence structures lacked political leadership and guidance, and some had been infiltrated by criminal elements (Marks & McKenzie, 1998).

The actions of the members of these structures became increasingly unaccountable and problematic. Despite the very tenuous relationship between the ANC and the SDUs, the youth who belonged to these structures continued to view themselves both as comrades and defenders of the community. But their actions were often insidious. There was a 'new dominance of criminal, and often gang-related, activity under the aegis of community protection' (Raditapole & Gillespie, 1994: 11).

As we have already seen in Chapter 7, SDUs were also active in Diepkloof, and some of the members of these units have subsequently been found to be involved in very shady activities. In September 1991, Percy Mhlongo, a former member of the Diepkloof SDU, applied to the Truth and Reconciliation Commission for amnesty. At the time he was serving a 20-year jail service for the murders of a policeman and a Diepkloof resident, Jeremiah Mkhwanazi, whom Mhlongo claimed was a gangster. Mhlongo had previously been convicted of housebreaking and theft while he was an SDU member. He admitted that, in shooting Mkhwanazi, he had acted against his commander's instructions (*South African Press Association*, 1 September 1999).

In another case, Morris Zakhele Nkosi applied for amnesty for the killing of two men during a robbery. Nkosi testified to the Truth and Reconciliation Commission that he was a member of the 'street' defence unit in Diepkloof, and had been a card-carrying member of the ANC. He had never attended any ANC meetings in Diepkloof. Amnesty was denied. The Commission felt it was 'highly improbable' that a SDU would instruct a new recruit to handle a pistol and to enact a robbery. The important point, however, is that Nkosi defined and declared himself member of the ANC and an active member of the local ANC-aligned defence unit which he claimed to have joined in early 1991.◊

These two cases serve to corroborate the findings of this book. In Diepkloof, and no doubt in other townships throughout the country, political youth organisations witnessed a real decline in the early '90s. Many who joined for the first time were inexperienced, unaccountable, and were not schooled in the discipline and ideology of the youth organisations of the '80s. The collective activities (both violent and peaceful) of the comrades became less directed and exemplary. The integrity of the youth social movement suffered as a result, and proper organising and mobilising became increasingly difficult as the '90s marched on. But this is not the whole story. These problems are compounded by the fact that the Diepkloof youth continued to see violence as a justifiable tactic in achieving 'political' objectives in the early '90s. They also continued to view themselves as having a moral advantage that, in itself, served to legitimate a whole range of activities.

■ *Has South Africa lost all those youth who actively defended their communities, who triumphed over those who engaged in criminal activities, and who dreamed of a real democracy?*

The comrade identity remained strong in the early '90s, despite the fact that their social movement had been undermined and their role as change agents diminished. The youth continued to strive for equality and peace and to see their contribution as valuable. At the local level, in places like Diepkloof, they continue to fight crime and the scourge of AIDS. Many thousands of youth, from Diepkloof and other townships, have made use of their experiences and training in the Charterist Youth Movement to further improve the life all South Africans. Today they hold important and responsible positions in government, the private sector and in non-government organisations.

Some township youth, who saw themselves essentially as local youth activists, were elected or appointed to key positions in government. Their discipline, commitment to democracy, heightened education, and skills in dealing with a broad range of people – all developed as youth activists – made them excellent candidates for responsible government posts. Journalist Makoni Ratshitanga was particularly fascinated by the turn of events in the life of

---

◊ Information found on the website of the Truth and Reconciliation Commission (http://www.truth.org.za/decisions/1999/ac990200.htm).

Paul Mashitile, who in the '80s was a local leader of the Alexandra Youth Congress. In 1998, Mashitile was appointed Minister for Safety and Security in Gauteng. Ratshitanga writes that:

> way back in 1987, while in detention at the small Jeppestown police station, Paul Mashitile never imagined that his jailers would one day have to account to him. Nor did the police themselves in those turbulent days think of being led by a township activist. (*Mail & Guardian*, 9 April 1998)

There are similar cases of success from Diepkloof. A number of members of the 1985 Detachment of activists in Diepkloof have moved from local township comrades to public positions of influence. Makgane Thobajane, or Bob Marley as he was fondly known in Diepkloof, is currently working for the Greater Johannesburg Metropolitan Council. He is appointed there as the Labour Relations Specialist, dealing with the difficult interface of the public sector trade unions and the Metropolitan Council as employer. Makgane now lives with his wife and three children in Kempton Park. He maintains strong links with the comrades and community of Diepkloof whom he visits regularly.

Musa Manganyi, alias Namedi, was elected as a local councillor for the Greater Johannesburg area. He fulfilled this role for five years, mainly dealing with the difficult issue of transport. As a result of his competence and commitment, he was offered a post as manager of a bus company in July 2000. Despite his upward mobility, Musa continues to live with his extended family in Diepkloof, although he is planning to get married in the near future. He is in regular contact with many of the young people who were members and supporters of the Charterist youth movement organisations in the '80s and early '90s. William Makgomata is a third member of the 1985 Detachment who comes to mind immediately. He is currently a senior consultant at Arthur Anderson, a prestigious law and accounting firm.

But not all the comrade youth of Diepkloof have become either 'heroes' or 'villains'. In August 2000, I decided to try to find out what had happened to the other young comrades who form the voices of this book. I could not track down the details of each one of them. In general, the young comrades from the '80s and early '90s were still in Diepkloof. Many of them were not employed on a full-time basis. They moved between a series of temporary jobs trying to 'live in a decent way'. A few had been implicated in criminal activities, but they were the minority by far. They aspired to live lives as young adults with meaningful jobs, allowing them to be responsible parents and family members.

Lilian still lives in Diepkloof. She is a member of the South African Police Service where she mainly deals with investigative tasks. She loves her job. She is married and has a young child. Thandeka still lives in People's Village, one of the squatter camps in Diepkloof. She is happily married with one child, and assists her husband who is self-employed.

Sipho is employed full time with Telkom. He has distanced himself somewhat from the political structures in Diepkloof. He is drug dependent. Friends and comrades like Namedi have tried to help Sipho with his drug problem, but have been unsuccessful. Sipho continues to live in Diepkloof. Zola has returned to South Africa and to Diepkloof. He has joined the South African National Defence Force, but still believes that black South Africans are oppressed and that the revolution should continue. He is in the process of buying a house.

Musi was shot and killed in 1998 when his car was hijacked. At the time of his death, he was employed by the National Health and Education Workers' Union. He also conducted research on a contract basis for the Department of Education. He had got married shortly before his death. Thami also lives in Diepkloof and works full-time at Woolworths.

■ *Why did some Diepkloof youth 'make it', while others did not?*
Youth such as Makgane and Musa, on the face of it, are like any other young people who grew up in Diepkloof prior to the transition to democracy. They came from working-class families. They attended local schools and had no tertiary education – in fact, Musa did not complete high school. They were not networked into the corporate sector. But they were both dedicated leaders of the Charterist youth movement in Diepkloof. They were schooled informally in the organisations of this movement where they gained insight into the concepts of power and inequality, and theorised about how societies function and how they change – something most young adults only learn on attending university. They acquired life skills such as how to administer mass organisations, how to manage large groups of people, how to negotiate between differing interest groupings, and how to mediate conflict.

As leaders, particularly during the '80s, they understood the real meaning of discretion, integrity and responsibility. The decisions they made often carried with them serious consequences and implications. They knew how to network and how to develop the trust of community members of all ages. This array of skills and knowledge, together with a proven record of integrity and exceptional discipline, meant that they could make a valuable contribution to most organisations or institutions. Having been leaders in their community, they were also known in Diepkloof and beyond. In a way, being leaders of the organisations to which they belonged, provided them with social mobility denied most township youth of their generation. They did not participate in the liberation movement with this purpose in mind, but the movement provided them with an unexpected opportunity to move beyond the confines of township realities. Vuyani, no doubt, as a respected and much admired youth leader, would also have been one of Diepkloof's shining stars.

## So, did Vuyani die in vain?

Vuyani died, in his own words, 'a proud soldier of the liberation movement'. The struggle he died for achieved its broad purpose – the political freedom of all South Africans. His life and death inspired many hundreds of youth in Diepkloof and throughout Soweto to be active members of political organisations, and to play a role in shaping their own destiny. He was a leader of a social movement that celebrated discipline, knowledge, courage and commitment. Many of the youth who were touched by Vuyani's guidance continued to cherish these values long after he died, despite the difficult conditions that they confronted in their daily lives.

Vuyani died with 'no regrets', but he did hope for a 'Communist future'. He would most probably be saddened that South African society is still not characterised by equality or economic justice, and that a host of 'new' social issues now confront the youth of South Africa, such as crime, HIV/AIDS, and unemployment. Still, Vuyani, and the others who died in the prime of their lives, did not die in vain. They set the scene for a new generation of youth who will not know formal apartheid, brutal repression, or the fundamental denial of human rights.

# Theorising about Diepkloof youth

This book is underpinned by social movement theory. It seemed appropriate, therefore, to provide a short and simplified appendix outlining this theory and the way in which it was used in this book. This chapter is by no means a comprehensive account of the vast array of theorisations of social movements, but is instead an introductory account.

Theories about social movements and collective action are beset by polemics and a number of intractable problems. They are also characterised by attempts to describe, rather than explain, social movements. Theorists constantly come up with new ways of understanding social movements, and of attacking existing theoretical starting points and assumptions. This has led Scott to ask if sociological interpretation of social movements should 'be motivated exclusively by the search for novelty?' (1990: 156). Similarly, Charles Tilly believes analysing collective action is a 'risky venture ... For one thing, there are too many experts around ... the determined students of collective action run the risk of labelling the obvious' (1978: 5).

Social movements, Tilly argues, are characterised by collective action which he defines as those actions in which groups of individuals '[act] together in pursuit of common interests'. But, other theorists emphasise other aspects of social movements. Some theorists emphasise structure, others agency. Some emphasise class, others diversity in status. Some emphasise collective interest, others environment. Some emphasise the newness of contemporary social movements, others their continuity with older movements. Scott's definition is probably the most all-encompassing. He says social movements involve:

> ... a collective actor constituted by individuals who understand themselves to have common interests, and for at least some significant part of the social existence, a common identity. Social movements are distinguished from other collective actors in that they have mass mobilisation, or a threat of mobilisation as their prime source of ... power. They are further disassociated from other collectivities such as voluntary associations or clubs, in being chiefly concerned to defend or change society or the relative position of one group. (1990: 6)

# Debating social movement theory

Many of the key modern debates around social movements emerged in the '70s. These were mostly a response to earlier understandings of 'traditional' social movements, centring around class and nation. The two key traditions that are reckoned with are those of Marxian or Durkheimian origin.

Early Marxists are asked by modern theorists such as Charles Tilly whether all collective action is to be understood by identifying the class base of organisation and leadership. For Marx, society was divided into classes that had particular interests. Marxists after Marx continued to assert that collective action was based on material conditions. However, most modern theorists – even neo-Marxists such as Castells – agree on the need to move beyond posing structuralism and class struggle as the main determinants of social change.

A second critique of the early Marxists is that they are unclear about whether explanations are best based on 'structure' or 'agency'. For Melucci, quoted in Scott, the debate is between those who focus on structural contra-dictions and crises as giving rise to social movements, and those who stress shared beliefs and orientations. Theorists in the '70s broke out of these duali-ties. Touraine and Habermas, for example, both looked at the link between forms of conflict and the emerging structure of post-industrial society.

Hyslop and Bundy, quoted fairly extensively in the early chapters in this book, are two theorists of South African youth social movements who would classify themselves as Marxist. Their explanations of these social movements are concerned largely with the socio-economic 'conjunctural' in which they emerge. Seekings, partly in response, wisely warns that the youth, among others

> ... need to be treated as actors in a meaningful sense, and not simply as the bearers of structural conditions such as education, employment or political crises. Neither political behavior nor violence can be explained solely in terms of underlying struc-tural conditions ... (1996: 16)

While the classical Marxists came under attack from the new social move-ment theorists in the '70s, most were more concerned with contesting Durkheimian or 'classical' theorists' accounts of social movements. These theories, dominant until the early '60s, adopted the socio-psychological tradi-tion, together with ideas of 'mass society' proposed by Smelser, among others.

The classical model generally had a causal sequence, which accounted for the rise of social movements. There were a number of assumptions that underpinned this approach. First, it distinguished between institutional and non-institutional collective behaviour. The former was seen to be 'normative', the latter was not. Second, it saw social movements as resulting from societal breakdown or institutional change that gave rise to discontent, frustration and anger which, in turn, gave rise to collective action. Third, the model assumed that social movements and collective action were open to causal analysis. Fourth, it focused on the individual in looking at grievances and values as a response to social change.

There are fundamental problems with this model. The assertion that there is a simple one-to-one correspondence between strain and collective process is not sufficient. One needs to understand the political context in which social movements arise, and the balance of political power. A second problem is that it refers to actors of collective action as having 'abnormal psychological profiles'. Yet these profiles are inferred from objective rather than subjective data.

The Durkheimian approach to understanding social movements – particularly of the youth – remains popular in South Africa. However, it has been challenged both in South Africa and internationally. South African sociologist Ari Sitas, for example, has stated that social movements do not simply emerge as a result of social breakdown. They are, he says, the result of collective power which is neither reflexive nor spasmodic. Rather, he says, social movements are challenges to social orders and are best 'studies through the voices and discussions of those who constitute collective nuclei of participants, formal or informal, within such movements' (1992: 629).

The inadequacies of the classical approaches became clear in the '60s and '70s when massive social movements began to emerge in Europe and the United States that were not solely a response to economic crisis and breakdown. Blacks, students, workers and other groups struggled to effect basic changes in the economic and social structures of society. These responses could not be called irrational. New theories were developed which argued that social movements were normal and participants were rational, well-integrated members of organisations.

In the emerging literature, Cohen (1985) – among others – identified three main approaches to collective action: the 'resource mobilisation' approach, the 'identity-oriented' approach, and the 'political process' approach. I believe these 'boxes' are a little too distinct. Still, let us examine them briefly.

### ■ *The resource mobilisation approach*

Resource mobilisation theorists reject the psychological emphasis, the 'breakdown' theory and the economic determinism of traditional Marxists. They view participants of social movements as 'rational actor[s] employing strategic and instrumental reasoning, replacing the crowd as a central referent for the analysis of collective action' (Cohen, 1985: 674).

These theorists examine internal workings, organisation-building, resources needed, political opportunities, as well as tactics and strategies, in accounting for large-scale mobilisation. Some resource mobilisation theorists, such as Zald and McCarthy, believe the poor are in a weak position to bring about social change because of their lack of resources and are hence dependent on sponsors for help. It is useful to read Cohen, who distinguishes between Zald and McCarthy's approach which focuses on questions of management and financing of social movement organisations, and Tilly, who focuses on questions of interest, opportunity, structures and mobilisation, as well as those of group structure and management.

Some South African social scientists make use of aspects of the resource mobilisation approach. Johnson (1989) is concerned with examining how youth organisations operate internally. He looks at how they have changed and their employment of various strategies and tactics. He considers the importance of leaders, pamphlets and newsletters as necessary resources for effective mobilisation and control over membership. Bundy's (1987) approach to the workings of youth organisations in the Western Cape in 1985 is similar. Bundy explores how a number of youth organisations that identified with the Charterist movement worked together and formed what the resource mobilisation approach would denote a 'social movement industry'.

Several problems have been raised with the resource mobilisation approach. For some, the approach remains unclear about why individuals act rationally in pursuit of interests in groups. For others, the theory does not adequately differentiate between change efforts made by excluded groups and those made by established polity members. It assumes, it is suggested, that the 'disadvantaged' require assistance from 'the elite' in effecting change and implies that elites are willing sponsors of social insurgencies. Proponents of this theory are also challenged for failing to acknowledge the political capabilities of the movement's mass base and for having no clear definition of the resources needed. The gaps in this approach make it necessary for social movement theorists to:

(a) look into the processes by which collective actors create the identities and solidarities they defend, (b) assess the relations between adversaries and the stakes of their conflicts, and (c) analyse the structural and cultural developments that contribute to such heightened reflexivity (Cohen, 1985: 31).

Charles Tilly is generally acknowledged as a social movement theorist of this school who has succeeded in overcoming some of these limitations. Hunt (1984: 244), for example, believes Tilly is concerned with how ordinary people come together to defend and organise themselves. He states that, for collective action to take place, people need to define themselves as having common interests. They also need to have a common identity and network to constitute organisation. At the same time, however, Tilly is sceptical about the extent to which one can rely on people's 'own utterances' in developing an understanding of collective action. People, he argues, are often unaware of their own interests, and may say conflicting things or nothing at all. It is therefore important, Tilly argues, to look at the internal workings of organisations, as well as at the political structures and opportunities that motivate and transform collective action.

## ■ The identity-oriented paradigm

For these theorists, who include Touraine, the identity of the actor needs to be understood to establish the costs and benefits of collective action and appropriate strategies and tactics. For Touraine particularly, participants in social movements need to 'tell' how they constitute a social movement and how, through their engagement, the identity of the social movement is constructed. This derives from his view that the problem with resource mobilisation theory is that it studies strategies, assuming that the actors are defined by their goals, and not by their social interactions. Touraine is concerned with examining the actors of social movements, both as people involved in structural conflicts and as cultural beings. His methodological approach is a hermeneutic one, which examines the self-understandings and ideologies of social movements.

Cohen, however, is critical of Touraine because he 'takes the false step of excluding strategic interaction from the concept of a social movement' (1985: 705). The main problem with Touraine's approach, he says, is that it tends to be a non-social account of collective action in that '... both actors and analysts who focus exclusively on the dynamics of identity formation tend to veer off the map of social movements' (ibid: 686).

In other words, approaches like Touraine's conflate the identity of the individual participant with that of the social movement. Identity-oriented theorists tend to ignore the key contributions of the resource mobilisation theorists who look at the problems of mobilisation, organisation and resources, as well as at political opportunities and threats.

In the '80s and early '90s, there was a general lack of research dealing with the question of identity in understanding youth social movements in South Africa. Seekings thus concluded that 'there is a clear need for research into the self-perceptions of youth, and into the views of youth held by other people on the ground' (1993: 23). Only when research like this is complete might it be possible to reconstruct the category of youth in ways that better combine observers' and participants' views, he says. This book is an attempt to take up the methodological challenge posed by Seekings in understanding social movements.

### ■ The political process model

This model examines external opportunity structures, such as the development of Bantu education in South Africa, regime crises – including the states of emergency, and state attempts to obstruct processes of collective action. Theorists such as Joppke (1991) are primarily concerned with the political context in which social movements emerge, and the consequent effects these social movements have on the political environment. Political process model theorists argue that the resource mobilisation theorists fail to assess the relationship of social movements to institutional political processes.

McAdam (1982) would probably situate some of Tilly's work within this approach, while stating that even Tilly does not deal adequately with the issue of political power. This, he feels, is the result of the distance between sociology and politics as two distinct disciplines each attempting to understand social movements.

The political process model argues that the existing polity is conservative by nature and will resist loss of power and major change. It believes existing polities, rather than supporting social movements, will seek to prevent unrepresented groups from developing solidarity. Social movements consequently need to be examined as generators – a series of dynamic exchanges with the socio-political environment they hope to transform. Further, this approach provides an inroad to understanding how social movements transform over time in terms of goals, strategies and organisational capacity.

Castells could perhaps also be described as a political process theorist. In his later work, he makes an important break with traditional Marxism. He asserts that class base and structural conditions cannot be seen as determining in understanding urban social movements. He is primarily concerned with the struggles of local urban residents around issues of 'collective consumption' such as health, education and housing. He sees social movements as contributors to structural changes and creators of new 'social meaning' of urban life and space. He believes urban social movements need to remain independent of political parties in order to effect social change.

Castells' approach is often used in explaining the upsurge of collective action by township youth in the '80s. An example of this approach can be found in Kumi Naidoo's (1992) examination of the rise of youth resistance in

Natal, as well as Seekings' (1993) account of the rise of township resistance. Both argue that township resistance began as a response to problems with the built environment and to grievances about education, rents and services.

There are a number of problems with Castells' approach. He does not look at the importance and nature of social bases in the mobilisation process. He also over-emphasises the capacity of social movements to bring about funda-mental change. However, he does provide a series of questions about local government and the struggle over urban resources as a major focus for local mobilisation of social movements.

# The 'new social movements'

'New social movement' theorists from the '70s are Habermas, Touraine and Melucci. They mainly look at the peace, feminist and ecological movements that emerged in what they call the post-industrial and post-modern eras. These movements, it is argued, differ significantly from the more 'traditional' social movements that organised around class and national issues. Actors in the new social movements, it is believed, are not identifiable in socio-economic terms, but on the basis of 'identity'. Participants act together since they iden-tify with a common social concern. These movements:

> ... target the social domain of 'civil society' rather than the economy or the state, raising issues concerned with the democ-ratisation of structures of everyday life and focusing on forms of communication and social identity. (Cohen, 1985: 667)

In objective terms, the base of these social movements consists largely of the 'new middle class' which has grown as post-industrial society has developed. The social base is generally young and has a high level of formal education. While 'old' social movements had identifiable class projects linked to shifts and crises in the social order, 'new' social movements are symbolic and moral, and have the potential to be apolitical. They are concerned with bringing about new lifestyles that stress equality, individual self-realisation, participation and human rights. They aim to transform the environment in terms of culture, language and habit. They construct reality rather than form a part of reality. In this view, in order to understand social movements, it is important to ex-amine three inter-relating factors – the identity of the actor, the definition of the opponent, and the field of conflict.

Advocates of new social movements have been criticised by other theo-rists who ask: What is 'new' about the new social movements? Some critics go so far as to call these new social movements 'moral crusades' or 'political pressure groups', and state that social movements are alien to the middle class (Eder, 1985). Critics say the conception of the new social movements is most unhelpful in the context of underdeveloped or Third World countries, where 'post-modernity' cannot be said to have arrived (Arrighi et al, 1989).

What theorists of new social movements do provide, however, is a reminder of the need to account for the manner in which major structural changes affect the nature of social movements – and of the need to grapple with the identities of these social movements and their actors.

# A suggested framework for understanding social movements

It is unproductive to set up the above paradigms as contesting approaches to understanding complex phenomena. What is needed is a synthetic approach that takes account of the positive contributions of these social theories in understanding social movements such as the Charterist youth movement in South Africa.

There seems to be no reason for the three main theoretical approaches to be seen as mutually exclusive. Social movements, I believe, cannot be understood in their entirety without taking account of the key insights of all of these approaches. All social movements emerge from within particular social and economic contexts. These environments provide both opportunities and constraints to social movements. The actors of social movements have shared interests, and social movements and their participants develop self-identities that shape collective action. And, all social movements require resources to be successful, as well as effective internal processes.

From my study in Diepkloof, I came up with a set of questions to help understand social movements. These questions, which were shaped by the research itself, are:

- Who are the youth that make up this particular social movement?
- What is their collective and individual consciousness and identity?
- What forms of collective action do they engage in, and why?
- What political structures and opportunities gave rise to this movement?
- What are the resources needed for these movements to exist and operate effectively?
- How do these movements transform with time?

# Ideology, consciousness and identity

To understand why social movements exist at all, it is important to understand the changes they hope to bring about in society. All social movements are characterised by a coherent set of ideas that their followers adhere to. They have an idea of the type of changes they would like to bring about, the type of society for which they are 'fighting'. Social movements have a particular set of ideas or ideology which is, what Touraine calls, an 'expression of collective will' (1990: 29). Social movement participants have a group consciousness or shared way of seeing the world. Ideology is highly fluid, given that there are always shifting rationales and changing circumstances within social movements (Goldstone, 1991).

How does the link occur between individual consciousness and identity and the 'group conciousness' so essential to collective action? To understand this, one needs to study collective action based on the 'self-analysis of militants' (Touraine, 1985). It is crucial to find out how participants define themselves as actors in the world. In the case of my study in Diepkloof, it was important to ask whether the 'militants' saw themselves as youth, comrades, men, the poor, or black – and what do these identities mean to them?

How does one 'recover the subject' in order to avoid treating subject groupings as 'the other'? We need to look at the particular forms of subjectivity, agency and experience of the dispossessed, consequently 'recovering' the subordinate from 'elitist' historiography (O' Hanlon, 1988). The process of identity formation involves the process of negation-violating symbols of the dominant. The identity of the 'subaltern' is not the same as the hegemonic identity (Said, 1988).

The understanding of identity formation of the 'subaltern' is not an easy one. There is a

> continuous struggle of the colonised to resolve the paradoxes which his displacement and dehumanisation of indigenous processes of identification sets up in his daily existence. (O' Hanlon, 1988: 205)

The challenge I faced was to attempt to understand the self-identity of participants of the Charterist social movement in Diepkloof; their 'self-analysis' of this movement; and the inherent and derived ideas that gave rise to their consciousness.

# Leaders, followers and organisations

What different types of people make up social movements? Who are the leaders, followers, activists, organisers, and so on?

It is important to understand that social movements are made up of groups of people with differing goals, motivation, expertise, understanding and commitment. Within any social movement there are always different groups of participants who have varying consciousness, discernment, and motivations for their involvement. These differences have an impact on the nature of collective action.

Zald and McCarthy (1987) also argue that we need to differentiate between constituents, adherents, bystanders and opponents. All people who benefit from social movements are termed 'potential beneficiaries', and social movements always try to mobilise both potential beneficiaries and non-beneficiaries in order to increase their social base.

Social movements do not only consist of a support base. To function effectively, they require organisations. Resource mobilisation theorists, particularly those who follow Zald and McCarthy, make an important distinction between social movements and social movement organisations. They say a social movement is a complex of formal organisation that identifies with and tries to implement the goals of a social movement. But while social movement organisations make up a social movement, the social movement itself may be larger than its constituent organisations. The distinction is an important one since it brings to our attention the people who identify with a particular social movement, yet are not members of any particular social movement organisation. These 'hangers-on', while important in terms of increasing the social base of any social movement, can bring with them a host of problems for social movements and their organisations. In particular, it is these 'hangers-on' who are most difficult to constrain during times of collective action.

Social movement organisations change during their life spans with the replacement of leadership, bureaucratisation, increasing radicalism and splits. They are subject to internal and external pressures that affect their visibility, structures, processes and ultimately their goals. They have to adapt to changing environments, and adaptation in turn may require changes in goals and in the internal arrangement of social movement organisations. These organisations may also lose members who feel their goals are not being achieved or if they become discredited.

The question of leadership is central to any social movement. Social movement organisations are often unstable, have few material incentives for members, and are non-routinised. Consequently, the success and failure of a social movement can be highly dependent on the qualities and commitment of leaders and the tactics they use. Loss of key leadership can lead to a decline in membership, to factionalism, and a lack of clear ideology and appropriate strategies and tactics. At the same time, however, the adequacy of leadership is itself contingent on the presence of an appropriate and strong organisational infrastructure.

To write this book I had to ask who were the participants of the Congress youth movement in Diepkloof; why they joined social movement organisations and participated in various forms of collective action; how their social movement organisations functioned; what role their leaders played; and what the consequences were of changes in leadership.

## Resources

Social movements, to be effective, need resources such as labour, materials, a means of communicating and money. The types of resources required depend on the nature of the struggle being waged. In the context of mass 'traditional' social movements, the most important resource is probably labour. None of the South African literature on youth social movements makes a concerted effort to examine what resources are available to a young, semi-literate, urban population, living in extreme poverty; and how resources, if any, are used.

Pamphlets, T-shirts, schools and literature are all resources used by youth movements. Where do they come from, and how do they facilitate mobilisation? Guns and other weapons are also 'resources' that have been made use of by these youth. What is their impact on the nature of social movements, and how does access to these resouces affect the tactics of youth social movements?

## Political opportunities and the social context

Social movements are conditioned by factors outside of themselves – they are social, economic and, more important for collective action, political. For people to take part in collective action and become participants in social movements, they need to feel that they will be able to effect change. They must believe that what can be gained from the action outweighs the possible negative consequences of their involvement.

Zald and Ash argue that the 'ideal condition for organisational growth is obviously a strong sentiment base with a low societal hostility toward the movement and its movement organisations' (1966: 55). In some instances, as this book shows, repression itself can lead to increased mobilisation and collective action. However, this is only the case when actors perceive the costs anticipated to be less important than the potential benefits of action.

A number of theorists of youth resistance in South Africa, following the tradition of Castells, stress the urban (or local) environment as an impetus for collective action and organisation. While local conditions and the built environment give rise to grievances and provide an entry point for collective action, political 'space' needs to be created for a wide expression of the collective will.

I had to explore the local conditions in Diepkloof for this book. I had to look at how political processes, including repression, affect organisation and mobilisation. How did comrade youth weigh up the costs and benefits of their engagement in a social movement? How did changes on the political terrain affect this social movement?

# Forms of collective action: strategies and tactics

Social movements choose a number of strategies and tactics to achieve their aims. The choice is dependent on a number of variables: the ideology; the form of organisation; and the political system within which the movement operates. Collective action is purposive, and even when spontaneous, it is rational.

According to Tilly (1978), groups tend to have repertoires of collective action: they may be competitive, reactive or proactive. 'Competitive' collective action lays claims to resources also claimed by rival or competing groups. 'Reactive' collective action occurs when people act in the name of threatened rights. 'Proactive' action makes claims that have not previously been exercised. The strategies and tactics of social movements alter as the political environment and organisations change. Targets of collective action are not indiscriminately selected.

Direct action is often resorted to when 'legitimate' action fails. In extreme situations, the movement will culminate in violent revolution. However, it is rational. Those who carry out acts of political violence do so as a conscious act. Collective violence is not simply the result of a society in crisis or a society that is unable to exercise influence. Collective violence is also generally not irrational and lacking in purpose. In fact, as Honderich (1976) maintains, violence can promote the desired ends of equality and democracy, and may even lead to improved life chances. Those who carry out collective violence do so as a conscious act (Parekh, 1972).

I believe collective violence emerges from other forms of collective action that are not intrinsically violent, such as meetings or peaceful protest. The rigid distinction between violent and non-violent collective action is a false one – the bulk of collective action stems from a greater stream of essentially non-violent action.

Collective violence usually results as a form of collective action in response to repressive actions of the state. It occurs when other legal avenues of protest have failed. Collective violence is a way of being heard and of expressing long-felt collective grievances. It often occurs when other forms of collective action have failed (Said, 1988). I have tried, in this book, to examine violent acts in terms of their own inner logic and rationality for those who carry out acts of collective violence.

The morality of the researcher, with regard to political violence, should not be the starting point in understanding political violence. Instead, what needs to be examined are the feelings and perceptions of perpetrators of violence, and the options (both violent and non-violent) that are seen as appropriate for reasonably achieving political ends. I have tried to situate youths' perceptions and discourse about political violence sociologically. I have tried to ask why youth activists made use of particular strategies and tactics. What were the inherent and derived ideas that informed these actions? How was collective and violent action organised? Who was involved in these various forms of collective action? Were there changes in the nature of collective action that accompanied organisational and political transformations?

# The career of social movements

Social movements and their organisations are not static. They change as their environment changes. It is essential to periodise – to put a date to – social movements. Any understanding of social movements should be dynamic – there should be a description of transition from one step to the next, and a representation of the interaction of parties in opposition or coalition. Social movements and their organisations undergo a variety of changes in terms of their goals, structure, tactics and strategies, and even their social base.

Changes in political terrain can give rise to a number of possibilities for social movements, according to Mainwaring and Viola (1984). They may be repressed by the state. They may become isolated and marginalised, leading to increased frustration and disappointment for participants and, consequently, apathy and sectarian radical opposition. They may be incorporated into the democratic system and lose their autonomy and their radical criticism. Finally, they may develop strong alliances with less radical elements.

Joppke (1991) believes social movements are dependent on public attention for the issues they address. Social movements feed on the external processes of agenda setting, which they reinforce but are unable to control. Shifts in public attention can trigger the decline of a social movement. Their bargaining strength, in relation to other groups in the political arena, is also a critical factor. To endure, social movements need to be able to withstand the response of elites, particularly repression. Perhaps most importantly, social movements have to create an enduring organisational structure in order to survive.

For me, the issue was how the Charterist youth movement changed from the '80s to the '90s. Why did these changes occur? What were the implications? Had the social movement 'declined' since the unbanning of the ANC and other political movements in February 1990?

# Conclusion

It is useless to set up straw men of social movement theorists and their varying approaches. It is far more constructive to examine what each approach has to offer in understanding particular social movements. While it is safe to assume that the classical approaches are inadequate, the resource mobilisation, political process model and identity-oriented theorists all have a contribution to make. It is impossible to understand social movements without studying their internal workings. It is equally impossible to understand social movements without comprehending the consciousness of participants and the identities they construct for themselves as participants. Finally, it is absurd to understand social movements outside of the context in which they emerge and exist – social, economic and political. The dynamic interaction of social movements and their environment is indispensable in understanding not only the emergence and life path of social movements, but also their effects on society, be they desired or unintended.

# The Freedom Charter

*Adopted at the Congress of the People, Kliptown, on 26 June 1955*

***We, the People of South Africa, declare for all our country and the world to know:***

That South Africa belongs to all who live in it, black and white, and that no government can justly claim authority unless it is based on the will of all the people;

That our people have been robbed of their birthright to land, liberty and peace by a form of government founded on injustice and inequality;

That our country will never be prosperous or free until all our people live in brotherhood, enjoying equal rights and opportunities;

That only a democratic state, based on the will of all the people, can secure to all their birthright without distinction of colour, race, sex or belief;

And therefore, we, the people of South Africa, black and white together equals, countrymen and brothers adopt this Freedom Charter;

And we pledge ourselves to strive together, sparing neither strength nor courage, until the democratic changes here set out have been won.

***The people shall govern!***

Every man and woman shall have the right to vote for and to stand as a candidate for all bodies which make laws;

All people shall be entitled to take part in the administration of the country;

The rights of the people shall be the same, regardless of race, colour or sex;

All bodies of minority rule, advisory boards, councils and authorities shall be replaced by democratic organs of self-government.

***All national groups shall have equal rights!***

There shall be equal status in the bodies of state, in the courts and in the schools for all national groups and races;

All people shall have equal right to use their own languages, and to develop their own folk culture and customs;

All national groups shall be protected by law against insults to their race and national pride;

The preaching and practice of national, race or colour discrimination and contempt shall be a punishable crime;

All apartheid laws and practices shall be set aside.

### *The people shall share in the country's wealth!*

The national wealth of our country, the heritage of South Africans, shall be restored to the people;

The mineral wealth beneath the soil, the banks and monopoly industry shall be transferred to the ownership of the people as a whole;

All other industry and trade shall be controlled to assist the wellbeing of the people;

All people shall have equal rights to trade where they choose, to manufacture and to enter all trades, crafts and professions.

### *The land shall be shared among those who work it!*

Restrictions of land ownership on a racial basis shall be ended, and all the land re-divided amongst those who work it to banish famine and land hunger;

The state shall help the peasants with implements, seed, tractors and dams to save the soil and assist the tillers;

Freedom of movement shall be guaranteed to all who work on the land;

All shall have the right to occupy land wherever they choose;

People shall not be robbed of their cattle, and forced labour and farm prisons shall be abolished.

### *All shall be equal before the law!*

No-one shall be imprisoned, deponed or restricted without a fair trial;

No-one shall be condemned by the order of any Government official;

The courts shall be representative of all the people;

Imprisonment shall be only for serious crimes against the people, and shall aim at re-education, not vengeance;

The police force and army shall be open to all on an equal basis and shall be the helpers and protectors of the people;

All laws which discriminate on grounds of race, colour or belief shall be repealed.

*All shall enjoy equal human rights!*

The law shall guarantee to all their right to speak, to organise, to meet together, to publish, to preach, to worship and to educate their children;

The privacy of the house from police raids shall be protected by law;

All shall be free to travel without restriction from countryside to town, from province to province, and from South Africa abroad;

Pass laws, permits and all other laws restricting these freedoms shall be abolished.

*There shall be work and security!*

All who work shall be free to form trade unions, to elect their officers and to make wage agreements with their employers;

The state shall recognise the right and duty of all to work, and to draw full unemployment benefits;

Men and women of all races shall receive equal pay for equal work;

There shall be a forty-hour working week, a national minimum wage, paid annual leave, and sick leave for all workers, and maternity leave on full pay for all working mothers;

Miners, domestic workers, farm workers and civil servants shall have the same rights as all others who work;

Child labour, compound labour, the tot system and contract labour shall be abolished.

*The doors of learning and culture shall be opened!*

The government shall discover, develop and encourage national talent for the enhancement of our cultural life;

All the cultural treasures of mankind shall be open to all, by free exchange of books, ideas and contact with other lands;

The aim of education shall be to teach the youth to love their people and their culture, to honour human brotherhood, liberty and peace;

Education shall be free, compulsory, universal and equal for all children;

Higher education and technical training shall be opened to all by means of state allowances and scholarships awarded on the basis of merit;

Adult illiteracy shall be ended by a mass state education plan;

Teachers shall have all the rights of other citizens;

The colour bar in cultural life, in sport and in education shall be abolished.

*There shall be houses, security and comfort!*

All people shall have the right to live where they choose, be decently housed, and to bring up their families in comfort and security;

Unused housing space shall be made available to the people;

Rent and prices shall be lowered, food plentiful and no-one shall go hungry;

A preventive health scheme shall be run by the state;

Free medical care and hospitalisation shall be provided for all, with special care for mothers and young children;

Slums shall be demolished, and new suburbs built where all have transport, roads, lighting, playing fields, creches and social centres;

The aged, the orphans, the disabled and the sick shall be cared for by the state;

Rest, leisure and recreation shall be the right of all;

Fenced locations and ghettoes shall be abolished, and laws which break up families shall be repealed.

*There shall be peace and friendship!*

South Africa shall be a fully independent state which respects the rights and sovereignty of all nations;

South Africa shall strive to maintain world peace and the settlement of all international disputes by negotiation – not war;

Peace and friendship amongst all our people shall be secured by upholding the equal rights, opportunities and status of all;

The people of the protectorates Basutoland, Bechuanaland and Swaziland shall be free to decide for themselves their own future;

The right of all peoples of Africa to independence and self-government shall be recognised, and shall be the basis of close co-operation.

Let all people who love their people and their country now say, as we say here:

**THESE FREEDOMS WE WILL FIGHT FOR, SIDE BY SIDE, THROUGHOUT OUR LIVES, UNTIL WE HAVE WON OUR LIBERTY.**

# BIBLIOGRAPHY

Adler, G. 1990. 'The politics of research during a liberation struggle: Interviewing black workers in South Africa'. In *International Annual of Oral History*. (Ed.) Grele, R. Westport, Cape Town: Greenwood Press.

Apter, D. 1990a. 'A view from the bogside'. In *The Elusive Search for Peace: South Africa, Israel and Northern Ireland*. (Eds.) Giliomee, H. and Gagiano, J. Oxford: Oxford University Press.

— 1990b. 'Towards a critical discourse on political violence'. In *Political Violence and the Struggle in South Africa*. (Eds.) Manganyi, M. and Du Toit, A. London: Macmillan Press.

Arrighi, G., Hopkins, T. and Wallerstein, I. 1989. *Antisystemic Movements*. London: Verso Press.

Bam, B. 1992. 'Introduction'. In *Faces in the Revolution: The Psychological Effects of Violence on Township Youth in South Africa*. (Ed.) Straker, G. Cape Town: David Philip.

Boraine, A. 1989. 'Strategies of the democratic movement'. In *Strategies for Change*. (Ed.) Fourie, S. Johannesburg: IDASA.

Bozzoli, B. 1991. *Women of Phokeng: Consciousness, Life Strategy and Migrancy in South Africa 1900-1903*. Johannesburg: Ravan Press.

Bundy, C. 1987. 'Street sociology and pavement politics: Aspects of youth and student resistance in Cape Town, 1985'. *Journal of Southern African Studies*, 13 (3).

— 1992. 'Introduction'. In *Black Youth in Crisis Facing the Future*. (Eds.) Everatt, D. and Sisulu, E. Johannesburg: Ravan Press.

Burgess, R. 1984. *In the Field: An Introduction to Field Research*. London: Unwin Hyman.

Byner, J. and Stribley, K. (Eds.) 1978. *Social Research: Principles and Procedures*. London: Open University Press.

Campbell, C. 1992. 'Learning to kill? Masculinity, the family and violence in Natal'. *Journal of Southern African Studies*, 18 (3).

Carby, H. 1982. 'White women listen! Black feminism and the boundaries of sisterhood'. In *The Empire Strikes Back: Race and Racism in 1970s Britain*.

(Ed.) CCCS. London: Hutchinson Press.

Carter, C. 1991. ' "We are the progressives": Alexandra Youth Congress activists and the Freedom Charter, 1983-85'. *Journal of Southern African Studies*, 17 (2).

— 1992. 'Community and conflict: The Alexandra Rebellion of 1986'. *Journal of Southern African Studies*, 18 (1).

Chaskalson, M. and Seekings, J. 1988. 'The challenge: From protest to people's power'. In *Political Conflict in South Africa – Data Trends*. Natal: Indicator Project South Africa, December.

Clingman, S. 1991. 'Introduction'. In *Regions and Repertoires: Topics in South African Politics and Culture*. (Ed.) Clingman, S. Johannesburg: Ravan Press.

Cock, J. 1991. *Colonels and Cadres: War and Gender in South Africa*. Cape Town: Oxford University Press.

Cohen, J. 1985. 'Strategies or identity: New theoretical paradigms and contemporary social movements'. *Social Research*, 52 (4).

Community Agency for Social Enquiry (Case) and Human Rights Commission (HRC). (Eds.) 1992. 'The reef violence: Tribal war or total strategy?' Unpublished report, March.

Dean, J. and Foote Whyte, W. 1978. 'How do you know if an informant is telling the truth?'. In *Social Research: Principles and Procedures*. (Eds.) Bynner, J. and Stribley, K. London: Open University Press.

Degenaar, J. 1990. 'The concept of violence'. In *Political Violence and the Struggle in South Africa*. (Eds.) Manganyi, N. and du Toit, A. London: Macmillan Press.

Deutscher, I. 1984. 'Asking questions'. In *Sociological Research Methods*. (Ed.) Blumer, M. London: Macmillan Press.

Dissel, A. 1997. 'Youth, street gangs and violence in South Africa'. Paper presented at the International Symposium on Youth, Street Culture and Urban Violence in Africa. Ivory Coast, 5-7 May.

Du Toit, A. 1990. 'Discourses on political violence'. In *Political Violence and the Struggle in South Africa*. (Eds.) Manganyi, M. and du Toit, A. London: Macmillan Press.

Eder, K. 1985. 'The "new social movements": Moral crusades, political pressure groups or social movements?' *Social Research*, 52 (4).

Edwards, R. 1990. 'Connecting method and epistemology: A white woman interviewing black women'. *Womens' Studies International Forum*, 13 (5).

Engelbrecht, S. 1991. 'The youth in education: Opportunities and threats'.

Paper presented to the Youth Seminar held by the Centre for Science Development, Pretoria.

Ferreira, M. 1988. 'The methodology of unstructured interviewing'. In *Introduction to Qualitative Research Methods*. (Eds.) Ferreira, M. et al. Pretoria: HSRC.

Foley, M. 1990. 'Organising ideology and moral suasion: Political discourse and action in a Mexican town'. *Comparative Studies in Society and History* (32).

Frank, C. and Fisher, S. 1998. 'Kids, drugs and transformation: Raising conceptual issues'. *Crime and Conflict*, (12).

Frankel, P. et al. (Eds.) 1988. *State, Resistance and Change in South Africa*. USA: Croom Helm.

Frederickse, J. 1990. *The Unbreakable Thread*. Johannesburg: Ravan Press.

Gamson, W. 1987. 'Introduction'. In *Social Movements in an Organisational Society*. (Eds.) Zald, M. and McCarthy, J. Oxford: Transaction Books.

Gibson, K. 1991. 'The indirect effects of political violence on children: Does violence beget violence?' Paper presented at the Centre for the Study of Violence and Reconciliation. Johannesburg.

Ginwala, F. 1992. 'Into and out of Codesa negotiations: The view from the ANC'. In *Peace, Politics and Violence in the New South Africa*. (Ed.) Etherington, N. London: Hans Zell Publishers.

Glaser, C. 1992. 'School, street and identity: Soweto youth culture 1960-1976'. Paper presented to the University of the Witwatersrand, Graduate Seminar.

Goldstone, J. 1991. 'Ideology, cultural frameworks, and the process of revolution'. *Theory and Society*, (20).

Grest, J. 1988. 'The crisis of local government in South Africa'. In *State, Resistance and Change in South Africa*. (Eds.) Frankel, P. et al. Pretoria: Signal Press.

Gurr, T. 1971. *Why Men Rebel*. New Jersey: Princeton University Press.

Habermas, J. 1991. 'New social movements'. *Telos* (49), Fall.

Hart, D. 1984. 'South African literature and the Johannesburg black urban townships'. M.A. dissertation. Johannesburg: University of the Witwatersrand.

Hartshorne, K. 1992. 'Education and employment'. In *Black Youth in Crisis Facing the Future*. (Eds.) Everatt, D. and Sisulu, E. Johannesburg: Ravan Press.

Hellman, E. 1962. *Soweto – Johannesburg's African City.* Johannesburg: South African Institute for Race Relations.

Honderich, T. 1976. *Three Essays on Political Violence.* London: Basil Blackwell.

Hunt, L. 1984. 'Charles Tilly's collective action'. In *Vision and Method in Historical Sociology.* (Ed.) Skocpol, T. New York: Cambridge University Press.

Hyslop, J. 1988. 'School student movements and state education policy: 1972-87'. In *Popular Struggles in South Africa.* (Eds.) Cobbett, W. and Cohen, R. London: James Curry.

— 1990a.'A destruction coming in: Bantu Education as response to social crisis'. Unpublished paper.

— 1990b. 'Schools, unemployment and youth: Origins and significance of student and youth movements'. In *Education: From Poverty to Liberty.* (Eds.) Nasson, B. and Samuels, J. Cape Town: Credo Press.

Indicator Project South Africa. 1988. *Political Conflict in South Africa – Data Trends.* Natal, December.

I R Information. 1990. *The South African Township Annual.*

Jeffrey, A. 1997. *The Natal Story: 16 Years of Conflict.* Johannesburg: South African Institute of Race Relations.

Johnson, S. 1989. ' "The soldiers of Luthuli": Youth in the politics of resistance in South Africa'. In *No Turning Back.* (Ed.) Johnson, S. Bloomington: Indiana University Press.

Joppke, C. 1991. 'Social movements during cycles of issue attention: The decline of the anti-nuclear energy movements in Germany and the USA'. *British Journal of Sociology*, 42 (1).

Kane-Berman, J. 1978. *Soweto: Black Revolt, White Reaction.* Johannesburg: Ravan Press.

Lebelo, M. 1988. 'Sophiatown removals: relocation and political quiescence'. Honours dissertation. Johannesburg: University of the Witwatersrand.

Leggett, T. 1999. 'Finding an age of reason for the young'. *Mail & Guardian*, 14 May.

Leggett, T., Moller, V. and Sotshongaye. 1997. 'Youth brigades of Natal? On the possibility of a national youth service programme'. *Indicator South Africa*, 14 (3).

Le Roux, P. 1991. 'The youth in the economy'. Paper presented at Youth Seminar held by the Centre for Science Development, Pretoria.

Letsebe, A. 1991. 'The contribution of youth clubs to national development'.

Paper presented at Marginalised Youth Conference convened by the Joint Enrichment Project, Broederstroom, June.

Lodge, T. 1985. *Black Politics in South Africa since 1945.* Johannesburg: Ravan Press.

— 1987. 'The United Democratic Front: leadership and ideology'. African Studies Institute seminar paper. Johannesburg: University of the Witwatersrand, August.

— 1991a. 'Introduction: Reform, recession and resistance'. In *UPDATE South Africa: Time Running Out: All Here and Now: Black Politics in South Africa in the 1980s.* (Eds.) Lodge, T. and Nasson, B. Johannesburg: David Philip.

— 1991b. 'The rise of the UDF'. In *UPDATE South Africa: Time Running Out: All Here and Now: Black Politics in South Africa in the 1980s.* (Eds.) Lodge, T. and Nasson, B. Johannesburg: David Philip.

— 1992. 'The African National Congress comes home'. African Studies Institute seminar paper. Johannesburg: University of the Witwatersrand, June.

— 1999. *Consolidating Democracy: South Africa's Second Popular Election.* Johannesburg: Witwatersrand University Press.

Lowe, S. 1986. *Urban Social Movements: The City After Castells.* London: Macmillan Press.

Mainwaring, S. and Viola, E. 1984. 'New social movements, political culture, and democracy: Brazil and Argentine in the 1980s'. *Telos* (61).

Management, Planning and Marketing Services. 1990. *Black Townships of the PWV: Special Report.* Johannesburg.

Mandy, N. 1984. *A City Divided: Johannesburg and Soweto.* Johannesburg: Macmillan Press.

Manyanyi, N. 1990. 'Crowds and their vicissitudes: Psychology and the law in the South African courtroom'. In *Political Violence and the Struggle in South Africa.* (Eds.) Manganyi, N. and du Toit, A. London: Macmillan Press.

Manganyi, N. and du Toit, A. 1990. 'Introduction: The time of the comrades'. In *Political Violence and the Struggle in South Africa.* (Eds.) Manganyi, N. and du Toit, A. London: Macmillan Press.

Marks, M. and McKenzie, P. 1998. 'Militarised youth: Political pawns or social agents?' In *From Defence to Development: Redirecting Military Resources in South Africa.* (Eds.) Cock, J. and McKenzie, P. Cape Town: David Philip.

Marks, S. and Trapido, S. 1992. 'Introduction'. *Journal of Southern African Studies*, 18 (1).

Mashabela, H. 1988. *Townships of the PWV.* Johannesburg: South African Institute of Race Relations.

Mattera, D. 1987. *Gone with the Twilight*. Johannesburg: Ravan Press.

McAdam, D. 1982. *Political Process and the Development of Insurgency*. Chicago: University of Chicago Press.

McKendrick, B. and Hoffman, W. 1990. (Eds.) *People and Violence in South Africa*. Cape Town: Oxford University Press.

Melucci, A. 1985. 'The symbolic challenge of contemporary movements'. *Social Research*, 52 (4).

Moikangoa, M. 1978. 'The effects of resettlement: Problems and potentials in Soweto'. Paper submitted to the Special Programme on Housing and Urban Development. London: University College, June.

Mokwena, S. 1991. 'The era of the Jackrollers: Contextualising the rise of youth gangs in Soweto'. Project for the Study of Violence seminar paper. Johannesburg: University of the Witswatersrand, October.

Moller, V. 1991. 'Lost generation found: Black youth at leisure'. *Indicator SA*, *'Issue Focus'*, May.

Molteno, F. 1987. 'Reflections on resistance – Aspects of the 1980 students' boycott'. *British Journal of the Sociology of Education*, 8 (1).

Morris, A. 1990. 'The complexities of sustained urban struggle: The case of Oukasie'. *South African Sociological Review*, 2 (2).

Morris, A. and Hyslop, J. 1991. 'Education in South Africa: The present crisis and the problems of reconstruction'. Unpublished paper.

Mouton, J. 1988. 'The philosophy of qualitative research'. In *Introduction to Qualitative Research Methods*. (Eds.) Ferreira, M. et al. Pretoria: HSRC.

Muller, J. and Cloete, N. 1987. 'The white hands: Academic and social scientists, engagement and struggle in South Africa'. *Social Epistemology*, 1 (2).

Murray, M. 1987. *South Africa: Time of Agony, Time of Destiny*. London: Verso Press.

Naidoo, K. 1992. 'The politics of youth resistance in the 1980s: The dilemmas of a differentiated Durban'. *Journal of Southern African Studies*, 18 (1).

Nekhwevha, F. 1992. 'The 1985 school crisis in the Western Cape'. Paper presented at ASSA Conference. Pretoria: University of Pretoria, June.

Nkululeko, D. 1987. 'The right to self-determination in research: Azania and Azanian Women'. In *Women in Southern Africa*. (Ed.) Quinta, C. London: Alison and Busby Limited.

Offe, C. 1985. 'New social movements: Challenging the boundaries of institutional politics'. *Social Research*, 52 (4).

O' Hanlon, R. 1988. 'Recovering the subject: Subaltern studies and histories of resistance in colonial South Asia'. *Modern Asian Studies*, 22 (1).

Olofsson, G. 1988. 'After the working class movement? An essay on what's new and what's social in the new social movements'. *Acta Sociologica*, 31 (1).

Oosthuizen, A. et al. (Eds.) 1979. *The Development and Management of Greater Soweto*. Johannesburg: Rand Afrikaans University.

Parekh, B. 1972. 'Liberal rationality and political violence'. In *Direct Action and Democratic Politics*. (Eds.) Benewick, R. and Smith, T. London: Allen and Unwin.

Parnell, S. 1990. 'The ideology of African home-ownership: The establishment of Dube, Soweto, 1946-1955'. History workshop seminar paper, Johannesburg, February.

Passerini, L. 1980. 'Italian working class culture between the wars: Consensus to Fascism and work ideology'. *International Journal of Oral History*, 1 (1).

Phillips, I. 1988. 'The opposition: After Kabwe and the emergency: Lessons from the 1980s'. In *Political Conflict in South Africa – Data Trends*. Natal: Indicator Project South Africa, December.

Pirie, H. 1984. 'Letters, words, worlds: The naming of Soweto'. Reprinted from *African Studies Journal*. Johannesburg: Witwatersrand University Press.

Posel, D. 1990. 'Symbolising violence: State and media discourse in television coverage of township protest, 1985-7'. In *Political Violence and the Struggle in South Africa*. (Eds.) Manganyi, N. and. du Toit, A. London: Macmillan.

— 1991. *The Making of Apartheid 1948-1961 – Conflict and Compromise*. New York: Oxford University Press.

Raditapole, T. and Gillespie, C. 1994. 'Proposal on Self-defence Units'. Unpublished paper.

Riordan, R. 1991. 'Marginalised youth: Unemployment as a characteristic of marginalised youth, and strategies for the creation of employment opportunities'. Paper presented at the Marginalised Youth Conference, Broederstroom, June.

— 1992. 'Marginalised youth and unemployment'. In *Black Youth in Crisis Facing the Future*. (Eds.) Everatt, D. and Sisulu, E. Johannesburg: Ravan Press.

Rive, L. 1980. *The Significance of Soweto*. Address to the annual general meeting of the National Development and Management Foundation. Johannesburg, November.

Robinson, J. n.d. a. 'A perfect system of control? State power and "native locations" in South Africa', mimeo.

— n.d. b. 'Administrative strategies and political power in South Africa's black townships, 1930-1960', mimeo.

Roth, J. 1980. *The Cult of Violence: Sorel and the Sorelians*. Los Angeles: University of California Press.

Rude, G. 1980. *Ideology and Popular Protest*. London: Lawrence & Wishart.

Rule, S. 1993. 'Propinquitous social diversity in Diepkloof, Soweto'. *South African Journal of Sociology*, (24).

Said, E. 1988. 'Identity, negation and violence'. *New Left Review*, (171).

Sapire, H. and Schlemmer, L. 1990. *Results of the Survey of 3 071 Black Households in the PWV*. Johannesburg: Urban Foundation.

Saul, J. 1991. 'The ANC put to the test'. *New Left Review*, (188).

Scharf, W. and Ngcokoto, B. 1990. 'Images of punishment in the people's courts of Cape Town, 1985-87: From prefigurative justice to populist violence'. In *Political Violence and the Struggle in South* Africa. (Eds.) Manganyi, N. and du Toit, A. London: Macmillan Press.

Schlemmer, L. 1991. 'An orientation to youth and politics in South Africa'. Paper presented at Youth Seminar of the Centre for Scientific Development, Pretoria.

Schrager, S. 1983. 'What is social in oral history?' *International Journal of Oral History*, 4 (2).

Schuurman, F. and Von Naerson, T. (Eds.) 1989. 'Introduction'. In *Urban Social Movements in the Third World*. New York: Routledge.

Scott, A. 1990. *Ideology and the New Social Movement*. London: Unwin Hyman.

Seekings, J. 1988. 'Political mobilisation in the black townships of the Transvaal'. In *State, Resistance and Change in South Africa*. (Eds.) Frankel, P. et al. Pretoria: Sigma Press.

— 1990. 'Quiescence and the transition to confrontation: South African townships, 1978-1984'. PhD thesis, Oxford University.

— 1992. ' "Trailing behind the masses": The United Democratic Front and township politics in the Pretoria-Witwatersrand-Vaal region, 1983-84'. *Journal of Southern African Studies*, 18 (1).

— 1993. *Heroes or Villains? Youth Politics in the 1980s*. Johannesburg: Ravan Press.

Segal, L. 1990. *Slow Motion: Changing Masculinity, Changing Men*. London: Virago Press.

Segal, L., Pelo, J. and Rampa, P. 1999. ' "Asicamtheni magents – Let's talks, Magents": Youth attitudes towards crime'. *Crime and Conflict*, (15) 1999.

Shubane, K. 1991. 'Soweto'. In *UPDATE South Africa: Time Running Out: All Here and Now: Black Politics in South Africa in the 1980s*. (Eds.) Lodge, T. and Nasson, B. Johannesburg: David Phillip.

Silas, D. (Ed.) 1968. *International Encyclopedia of the Social Sciences*. USA: Macmillan and Free Press.

Simpson, G. 1998. 'Urban crime and violence in South Africa'. In *Justice for Children*. (Eds.) Petty, C. and Brown, M. London: Save the Children.

Sitas, A. 1992. 'The making of the "comrades" movement in Natal, 1985-91'. *Journal of Southern African Studies*, 18 (3).

South African Communist Party (SACP). 1989. *The Path to Power: Programme of the South African Communist Party as Adopted at the Seventh Congress*.

South African Institute of Race Relations (SAIR). 1953. 'The Western Areas removal scheme'. Paper presented at the University of the Witwatersrand, Johannesburg.

Stadler, A. 1987. *The Political Economy of Modern South Africa*. Cape Town: David Philip.

Stanage, S. 1974. 'Violates: Modes and themes of violence'. In *Reason and Violence in Philosophical Investigations*. (Ed.) Stanage, S. London: Basil Blackwell.

Straker, G. 1992. *Faces in the Revolution: The Psychological Effects of Violence on Township Youth in South Africa*. Cape Town: David Philip.

Swilling, M. 1988. 'The United Democratic Front and township revolt'. In *Popular Struggles in South Africa*. (Eds.) Cobbett, W. and Cohen, R. London: James Curry.

Tilly, C. 1978. *From Mobilisation to Revolution*. New York: Random House.

— 1985. 'Models and realities of popular collective action'. *Social Research*, 52 (4).

Tilly, C., Tilly, R. and Tilly, L. 1975. *The Rebellious Century: 1830-1930*. Cambridge: Harvard University Press.

Touraine, A. 1985. 'An introduction to the study of social movements'. *Social Research*, 52 (4).

— 1990. *The Voice and the Eye: An Analysis of Social Movements*. New York: Cambridge University Press.

Urban Foundation. 1980. *Soweto*. Johannesburg.

Van Wyk, J. 1990. 'Nationalist ideology and social concerns in Afrikaans drama in the period 1930-1940'. History workshop seminar paper, Johannesburg, February.

Von Tonder, D. 1990. 'First win the war, then clear the slums: The genesis of the Western Areas scheme'. History workshop seminar paper, Johannesburg, February.

Williamson, J. et al. 1982. *The Research Craft*. Boston: Little Brown & Company.

Zald, M. and Ash, R. 1966. 'Social movement organisations: Growth, decay and change'. *Social Forces,* (44), March.

Zald, M. and McCarthy, J. 1987. 'Resource mobilisation theory'. In *Social Movements in an Organisational Society*. (Eds.) Zald, M. and McCarthy, J. Oxford: Transaction Books.

Zald, M. and Garner, R. 1987. 'Social movement organisations: Growth, decay and change'. In *Social Movements in an Organisational Society*. (Eds.) Zald, M. and McCarthy, J. Oxford: Transaction Books.

# Interviews

London, Mr. Official of the Diep-Alex administration in 1992, March 1992.

Mogadire, Mogamotsi. Youth activist and leader in Diepkloof in the '80s, January 1992.

Mogasi, Isaac. Prominent civic activist in Diepkloof in the '80s, February 1992.

Molefe, Themba. *Sowetan* journalist, December 1991.

Mothibe, Caiphus. Chairperson of Daveyton branch of Cosas, March 1992.

Motumi, Mr. Principal of Fons Luminous High School, July 1992.

Tedile, Busi. South African Black Social Workers' Association member and organiser of youth clubs in Soweto, July 1991.

Thobejane, Makgane. Youth activist and leader in Diepkloof in the '80s, February 1991.

Tloteng, Mr. Senior social worker with Nicro in Soweto, October 1991.

Zwane, Ashwell. Youth activist and leader in Alexandra in the early '80s, November 1991.

# INDEX